T0071198

Frame: MYKITA NO1 ALEXANDER | Photography: Mark Borthwick

Frame: MYKITA LITE TONA | Photography: Mark Borthwick

MYKITA

BERLIN | CARTAGENA | COPENHAGEN | LOS ANGELES | MONTERREY
NEW YORK | PARIS | TOKYO | VIENNA | WASHINGTON | ZERMATT | ZURICH

SHOP ONLINE AT MYKITA.COM

COMING SOON

The Kinfolk Entrepreneur

Featuring over 40 entrepreneurs, the latest in
Kinfolk's book series offers inspiration to anyone
forging their own professional path.

**Preorder now at Kinfolk.com.
In stores worldwide from October 2017.**

THE

KINFOLK

ENTREPRENEUR

IDEAS *for* MEANINGFUL WORK

NATHAN WILLIAMS

Made in Montréal

Photography by Arseni Khamzin

WWW.LUCCHESE.COM   AUSTIN • DALLAS • HOUSTON • NASHVILLE • SAN ANTONIO • SANTA FE

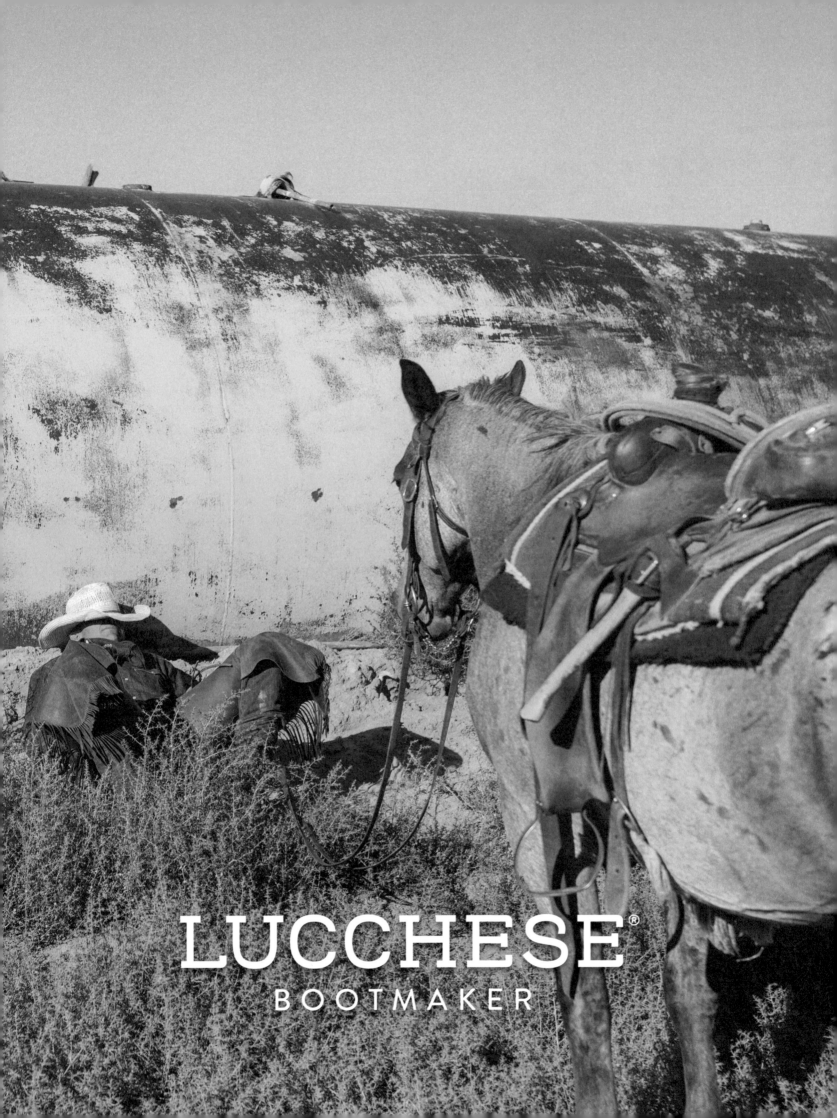

iittala.com

FLOYD

Furniture
for keeping.

The Floyd Bed.
Made in America.

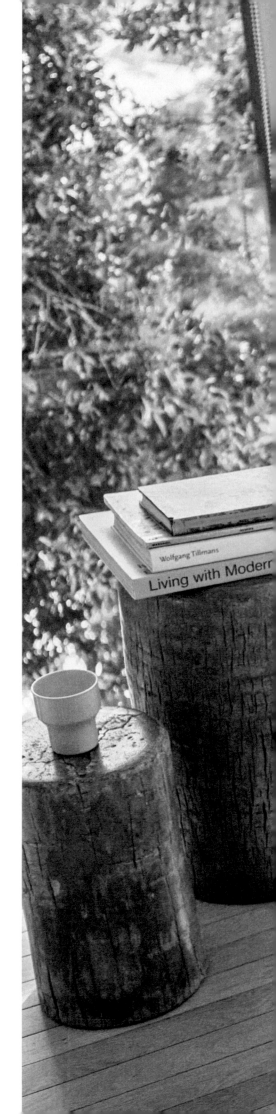

FLOYDDETROIT.COM

COCLICO

CONSCIOUSLY ARTFULLY ELEGANTLY

COCLICO.COM

KINFOLK

EDITOR-IN-CHIEF
Nathan Williams

EDITOR
Julie Cirelli

CREATIVE DIRECTOR
Anja Charbonneau

DEPUTY EDITOR
John Clifford Burns

DESIGN DIRECTOR
Alex Hunting

ASSISTANT EDITOR
Molly Mandell

CASTING DIRECTOR
Sarah Bunter

COPY EDITOR
Rachel Holzman

MANAGING DIRECTOR
Doug Bischoff

COMMUNICATIONS DIRECTOR
Jessica Gray

ADVERTISING DIRECTOR
Pamela Mullinger

PUBLISHING DIRECTOR
Amy Woodroffe

**SALES & DISTRIBUTION
DIRECTOR**
Frédéric Mähl

ACCOUNTING MANAGER
Paige Bischoff

STUDIO MANAGER
Monique Schröder

STUDIO ASSISTANT
Aryana Tajdivand-Echevarria

EDITORIAL INTERN
Mina Oh

CONTRIBUTING EDITORS
Michael Anastassiades
Jonas Bjerre-Poulsen
Ilse Crawford
Margot Henderson
Leonard Koren
Andrea Lippke
Hans Ulrich Obrist
Amy Sall
Matt Willey

ILLUSTRATION
Chidy Wayne

STYLING, HAIR & MAKEUP
Rebecca Alexander
Leandro Favaloro
Debbie Hsieh
Christopher Kam
Cyril Laforet
Martina Lucatelli
Giulia Querenghi
Fernando Torrent
Sarah Uslan
Terri Walker
Susan Winget
Yasuo Yoshikawa

PRODUCTION & SET DESIGN
Samuel Åberg
Lara Bonomo
Sam Jaspersohn
Brooke McClelland

WORDS
Alex Anderson
Lucy Ballantyne
Charles Bethea
Harriet Fitch Little
Sarah Moroz
Emily Nathan
Micah Nathan
Asher Ross
Tristan Rutherford
Charles Shafaieh
Nicola Twilley
Pip Usher
Molly Young

PHOTOGRAPHY
Akatre Studio
Michel Bonvin
René Burri
Daniele Fummo
Philippe Halsman
Emma Hartvig
Marsý Hild Þórsdóttir
John T. Hill
Leslie Kirchhoff
Fabien Kruszelnicki
Ricardo Labougle
Amber Mahoney
Katie McCurdy
Amara Nwosu
Francois Robert
Michikazu Sakai
Chris Schoonover
Jonathan Schoonover
Ferdinando Scianna
Zoltan Tombor
Michael Wilson
Pia Winther
Susan Wood Richardson

PUBLICATION DESIGN
Alex Hunting

ISSUE 25
All rights reserved. No part of this publication may be reproduced, distributed or transmitted in any form or by any means, including photocopying or other electronic or mechanical methods, without prior written permission of the editor, except in the case of brief quotations embodied in critical reviews and certain other noncommercial uses permitted by copyright law. For permission requests, write to the editor, addressed "Attention: Kinfolk Permissions," at the address below.

info@kinfolk.com
www.kinfolk.com

Published by Ouur Media
Amagertorv 14, Level 1
1160 Copenhagen, Denmark

The views expressed in Kinfolk magazine are those of the respective contributors and are not necessarily shared by the company or its staff.

SUBSCRIBE
Kinfolk is published four times a year. To subscribe, visit kinfolk.com/subscribe or email us at info@kinfolk.com

CONTACT US
If you have questions or comments, please write to us at info@kinfolk.com. For advertising inquiries, get in touch at advertising@kinfolk.com

Printed in Canada
by Hemlock Printers Ltd.

@LEVISMADEANDCRAFTED

LEVI'S®
MADE & CRAFTED®

ARTFUL CONSTRUCTION. ELEVATED DETAILS.
LEVI'S® BY DESIGN.

"Rejection is protection. I like to believe I'm wherever I need to be."
LOLA KIRKE – P. 54

Photograph: Zoltan Tombor

Tina Frey Designs
tinafreydesigns.com

"On weekends, I cook breakfast and lunch for everybody on my farm—whoever is hanging around gets fed."
MARTHA STEWART — P.123

Photograph: John T. Hill

ERIK
Jørgensen
THE MANUFACTURER

QUALITY AS A TOP PRIORITY

Erik Jørgensen Møbelfabrik was founded in 1954 in Svendborg, Denmark, by saddlemaker and upholsterer Erik Jørgensen. Erik Jørgensen's collection consists of well-known classics from Hans J. Wegner and Poul M. Volther as well as new furniture produced in collaboration with upcoming designers.

We aim to produce furniture that lasts. Not only for use but also to beautify our surroundings, and open our eyes to new ways of seeing and making furniture. A passion for design and good craftsmanship is what characterizes Erik Jørgensen Møbelfabrik.

WWW.ERIK-JOERGENSEN.COM

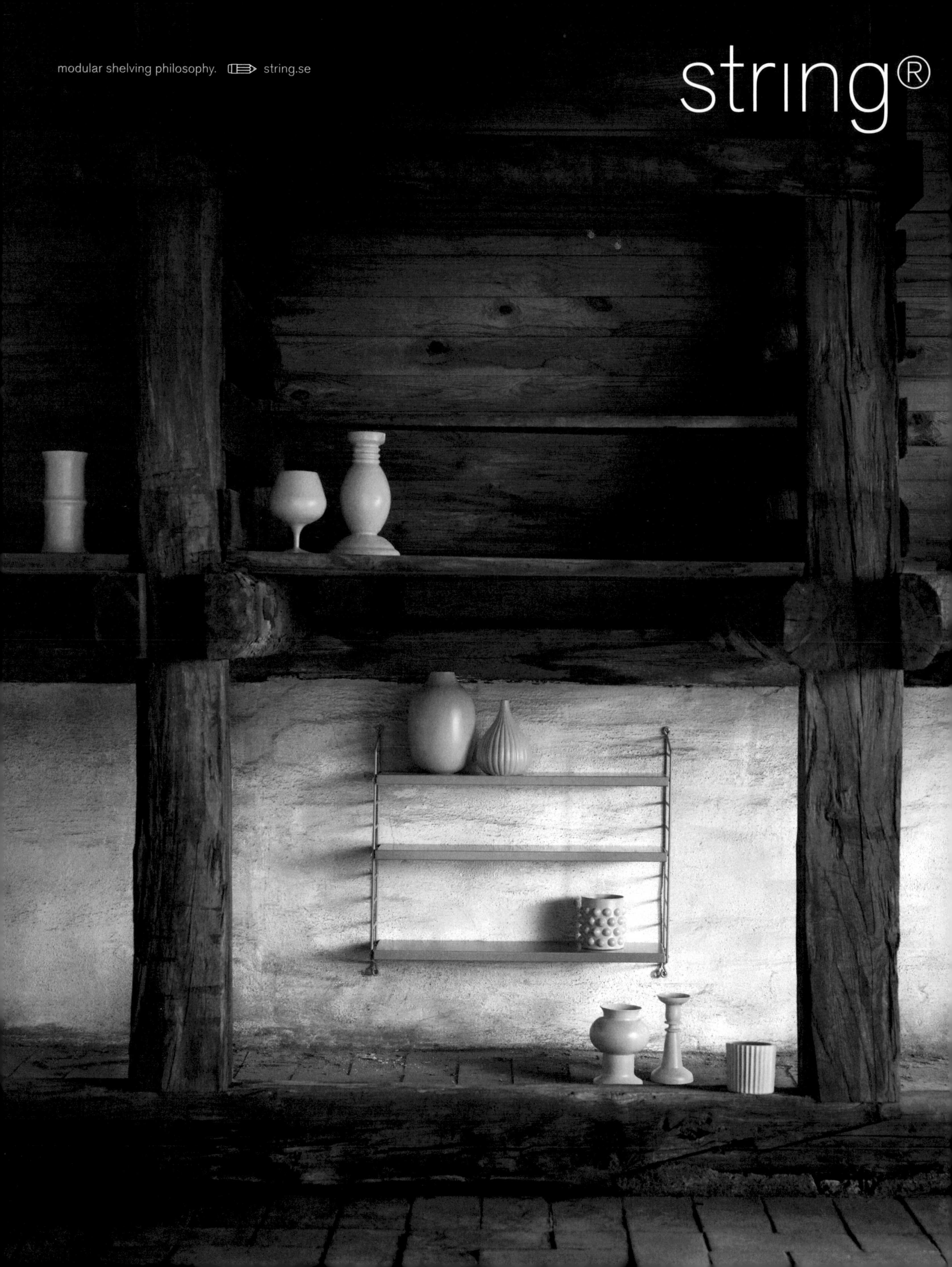
modular shelving philosophy. string.se
string®

Issue 25

Welcome

"There are few people alive with whom I care to pray, sleep, dance, sing, and (perhaps most of all, except sleep) share my bread and wine," begins M.F.K. Fischer's classic *An Alphabet for Gourmets.* In the first of a series of essays, Fischer describes how she learned to enjoy eating alone, capturing both the appeal and the taboo of dining solo (especially for a woman in 1949, when *Alphabet* was first published). "Sharing food with another human being is an intimate act, which should not be indulged in lightly," she concludes. Indeed, sharing food is one of the most primal acts we humans do, something that spans cultures and continents and yet is highly individual.

In this issue, we approach food as a lens through which identity and relationships can be interpreted. What does a person's approach to food tell us about their values? And how is food culture affected when values and communities shift? Freetown, Virginia, a town founded by emancipated slaves whose social glue was its tradition of sharing meals, was the childhood home of chef Edna Lewis. Long after Freetown disappeared, Lewis devoted her life to preserving the approach to food handed down from her mother and grandmother. On page 146, Lewis biographer Sarah Franklin explores why these traditions were worth saving.

Also in this issue, Martha Stewart discusses how she and Snoop bond over Gucci shoes and home cooking, and Alex Anderson deconstructs the Italian futurist movement's rejection of pasta in favor of food "tuned to high speeds." In *Cooking the Books* on page 158, we celebrate some decidedly non-essential food reading, from the electric terrines and microwaved hot dogs of '70s-era Betty Crocker to the Toffee and Pine Cones whipped up by Salvador Dalí. On page 167, we explore *The Book of Tasty and Healthy Food*, the 1939 soviet classic that offered up "dreamlike visions of the supposed fruits of communism." And on page 138, we present *How to Wrap Five Eggs*, a photo essay about the intricately stylized traditional Japanese method of food wrapping.

Elsewhere in the issue, Harriet Fitch Little investigates whether narcissism is truly a growing social concern or yet another way to silence people—young women, in particular—who express self-love in a public sphere. We meet rising actor Lola Kirke as she navigates the conventions of Hollywood. And we learn that mundane personal habits—like whether we tell dirty jokes or sing in the shower—reveal much about our characters. Luckily, when our quirks butt up against our significant other's quirks, we can take lessons from a couple's counselor on how to have better fights. "Good partners learn to seize on those small instances when concern, humor, even affection for the other person revive," writes Asher Ross on page 184. "Cultivate an appreciation for these moments and they may come more often."

JULIE CIRELLI

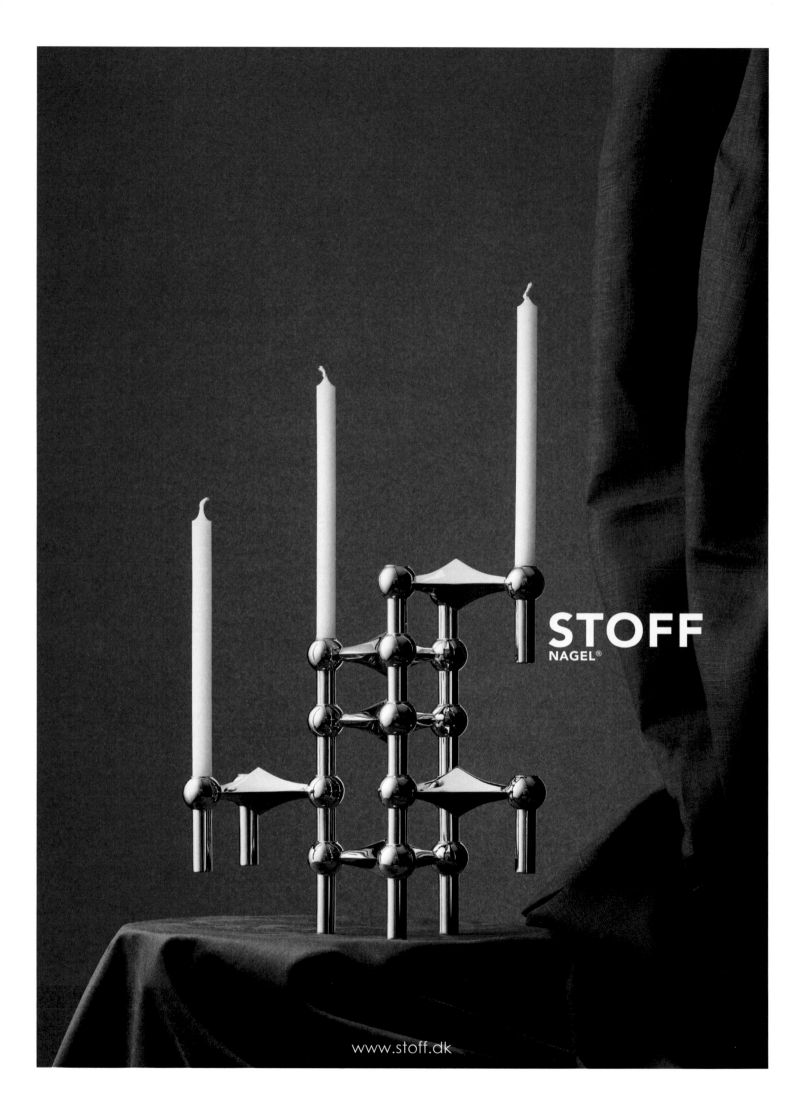

STOFF
NAGEL®

1
Starters

ALEX ANDERSON

Tick Tock

"Now" actually happened a split second ago:
A meditation on the passage of time.

Time flows: steady, unstoppable, invisible. The Greek philosopher Heraclitus imagined time streaming through existence, an inexorable medium of change. We understand it scientifically as a hidden background evident in the synchronized beat of clock hands or more precisely in the attosecond pulsing of beryllium ions. But our ordinary perception of time suggests that it is inconstant, elastic, rhythmic. Time flies; time drags on.

In moments of intense engagement—when conversation flows, when work gets done or when "fun" seems such an inadequate description—time moves in great, condensed chunks. By contrast, at a traffic light or in an anxious waiting room a plodding second hand expands time, marking ever widening, frustrating intervals. Time crawls, spreads out, and rises to thwart our plans.

It's easy to dismiss these varied perceptions as merely fanciful, or as evidence of humans' limited time-sense. After all, clocks keep rolling no matter what our feelings tell us. But this inconsistency has long perplexed philosophers and intrigued artists, particularly as modern science has managed to mark time ever more precisely.

We seem to occupy an instantaneous present that moves from the past toward the future, but what constitutes the present we feel, and how does it occupy time? Consider this simple event: A horse gallops by, 30 feet in front of you. You see the horse and hear it. Light bouncing off its head, mane and flanks reaches your eyes in about

0.000000033 seconds; the sound of its hooves reaches your ears in 0.27 seconds. You feel vibrations through your feet a bit later. Each of these impulses travels up shorter or longer neural pathways to your brain, which processes them and puts them in order. All of this seems to happen "now," but, considered precisely, it is already past. Physics and physiology never allow us to live in the present. Meanwhile, you smell plants and soil. You hear shivering blades of grass in a light breeze; you brush a fly off your forearm into the sunlight. An ambient "now" encompasses the "now" of the running horse.

The early 20th-century phenomenologist Henri Bergson described internal consciousness of time as a kind of personal duration. Everything we witness extends across time. This gives time different rhythms and densities that "measure the degree of tension and relaxation of different kinds of consciousness and thereby fix their respective places in the scale of being." The experience is so real for each of us, he argued, that we must consider it our primary measure of what happens.

In the context of experienced reality, homogeneous clock time, Bergson said, is "an idol of language, a fiction." This fiction appears, paradoxically, in the precise pioneering work of photographer Eadweard Muybridge, who settled a persistent question about the horse's gallop—whether all four hooves ever leave the ground simultaneously. The actual movement is so quick that human perception can't tell for certain.

Muybridge demonstrated with 24 bulky cameras capturing 24 successive instants that, yes, they do for an imperceptible, but recordable, moment. At the time, people found his images both informative and unsettling, because the cadenced frames caught the "truth" of the horse's awkward, imbalanced positions frozen in the midst of what is so evidently fluid, graceful movement.

Artists often take pleasure in exposing this variability of perceived time. Sculpture and literature seem especially suited to the effort. Myron's memorable *Discus Thrower*, sculpted in about 460 B.C., arrests the rotating arc of an Olympian's body, weight balanced, muscles rippling, and anticipates the release of the projectile. The extended event is not so much stopped, as compressed into bronze. Twenty-four hundred years later, in 1967, the Italian writer Italo Calvino, with similarly classical flair, checked a springing lion, poised hunter and launched arrow in *t zero*. Its 17 pages ponder the immanence of death or survival but end with the three objects perpetually suspended in an ellipsis. "In literature," Calvino says, "time is a form of wealth to be spent at leisure and with detachment."

Colloquial expressions about the inconstancy of time reveal a profound insight into its perplexing malleability in conscious experience. We know that perceived time builds its own consequential rhythms against the incessant, monotonous, illusory beat of hours, minutes and seconds.

Mechanical clocks behave nothing like the exquisitely precise quantum clocks that regulate our schedules, but all clocks demonstrate a flow of time at odds with our own elastic sense of how time moves.

Photograph © Philippe Halsman/Magnum Photos/Ritzau

A certain regard: the disorienting optical
art of a British painter.

SARAH MOROZ

Bridget Riley

Riley completed *Blaze 1*, shown
here, in 1962. There are five known
variations of the composition—a motif
that earned Riley the John Moores
Painting Prize in 1963.

British painter Bridget Riley's
work is a fascinating study of the
extremist possibilities of color,
line and shape. Hers is a woozy
spectral vision, immersive and
polarizing in equal measure. "Her
paintings don't merely hang on
the wall: they warp and pulsate,"
wrote art critic Jonathan Jones.
"What was she on when she came
up with her dangerous vision?"

Bridget Riley was born in South
London in 1931, and studied at
Goldsmiths and the Royal College
of Art. "The thing I discovered was
the healing power of looking," she
told the *Financial Times* in a 2014
interview about an exhibition of
her stripe paintings. She recount-
ed how her mother would "greet a
beautiful day, see it, point it out,"
in order to take her mind off of her
anxieties. Riley too adopted this
approach: "We were given sight.
I knew that somehow I wanted to
pursue this looking."

Riley taught at an art school
and worked at an advertising
agency during the first half of the
1960s, but gave up both gigs once
her dizzying and undulating paintings gained recognition. She
participated in group shows, including *The New Generation* at
the Whitechapel Gallery and
*Painting and Sculpture of a De-
cade (1954-1964)* at the Tate, both
in 1964. Riley also exhibited in
the 1965 New York show *The Re-
sponsive Eye*, which propelled the
concept of optical art into wider
discourse. In 1968, Riley won the
International Painting Prize at
the Venice Biennale for her work
at the British Pavilion with Phillip

King. She was the first British contemporary painter and, meaning-
fully, the first woman to be given
this award.

Commercial demand for Ri-
ley's work soared in the 1970s, but
it fell out of fashion by the 1980s.
It seems ironic that someone so
confrontational about optics lost
her own visibility on the art scene,
but she continued toiling in her
studio, directing the assistants she
employed to paint from her pre-
paratory notes. A slow resurgence
of exhibitions—a retrospective in
2003 at the Tate Britain in London,
then one in 2008 at the Musée
d'Art Moderne de la Ville in Paris—renewed public interest.

Riley's work is visually aggressive, forcing the viewer into direct
engagement, and many do not
care for aggressiveness, least of all
from female artists. Will Self wrote
a dismissive article in *The Independent* in 2008, deriding the "retinal
queasiness" she evoked. "Bridget
Riley's paintings are beautiful cre-
ations, but should they be regard-
ed as fine art—or merely framed
wallpaper?"

Indeed, her work creates an in-
tensity that manifests tangible effects of disorientation. (Jones went
so far as to say it "rearranges your
neurons.") Upon gazing at Riley's
work, the viewer is required to
grapple with their surroundings
anew precisely because it is flum-
moxing. This is an asset, not a bur-
den. Riley spent her career mining
a narrow field of visual expression,
but within those confines, she created something radical and play-
ful, swaying and disruptive.

Photograph © Bridget Riley 2017. All rights reserved.

Right photograph: Akatre Studio

EMOTIONAL BAGGAGE

by Molly Mandell

You may end up with more than just a backache if you overload your purse or backpack, according to a 2011 study published in the *Journal of Consumer Research*. Those toting a heavy load are prone to perceiving unrelated events as stressful. But, if not too heavy, a bag can be an intimate companion; it keeps our possessions safe while sticking by our side (quite literally) through the day-to-day. That notion hasn't slipped by Building Block, the Los Angeles–based accessories company founded by sisters Kimberly and Nancy Wu. The duo creates minimalist designs including the Book Wallet (top), Cylinder Duffel (middle) and Rucksack (bottom).

See Attached

Mementos and security blankets: Why some inanimate objects take on spiritual significance.

Intense connections to physical objects may seem antiquated during a digital era in which tangibility is increasingly devalued. Many of us, however, pepper our lives with inanimate things, be they items placed around the home or worn on the body. As dependent on the incorporeal cloud as someone may be, the thought of losing a family heirloom, Hand of Fatima pendant, wedding ring, or an otherwise unassuming object has the power to elicit worry and tears.

The security objects of early childhood are often the first step on a lifelong journey of building attachments to particular items. Many believe that these generally soft possessions, such as blankets and stuffed animals, serve as substitutes for the mother. Much like a parent, they too are considered singular and irreplaceable. In 2007, Bruce Hood of the University of Bristol designed an experiment in which 22 children between the ages of three and six were told that a complex-looking device they were shown could duplicate their "attachment" object. Only five took home "the copy."

This attitude is not just a facet of youth. Works of art created by specific people at specific points in time are popularly considered special in an unquantifiable way due to their aura, a quasi-spiritual essence that Walter Benjamin discusses in his essay *The Work of Art in the Age of Mechanical Reproduction*. Similar logic holds for tokens associated with a loved one, regardless of how replaceable or generic they may appear.

These emotion-filled objects often assume a metonymic character, embodying a relationship or singular experience while resting silently on a mantle or tucked away in a drawer. Souvenirs serve in part as mementos of entire events and places, just as other items represent various people, particularly those who have died. They're tied integrally to memories and relationships and, therefore, to our identities. Through them, we unshackle ourselves from the confines of body and mind, homes expand beyond their walls, and the past folds into the present. And as with a teddy bear, there is comfort in keeping alive what otherwise could be irretrievably lost.

www.jennifernewman.com

Showroom
8 Clerkenwell Green,
London, EC1R 0DE

Photography Oliver Perrott

AL FRESCO BENCH

The Korean approach to reading a room.

LUCY BALLANTYNE

Word: Nunchi

Language: Korean. *Pronunciation:* "Nun-she." *Etymology:* Translates literally from Korean to English as "eye-measure."

Meaning: Nunchi is the ability to subtly but incisively gauge the mood of the people around you. The concept is a central part of Korean culture—having it, or not having it, determines how graciously one moves through life. Someone who has nunchi is a *nunchi ppareuda*—they can intuitively sense the right or wrong thing to do or say in any given social situation. A *nunchi eopta* is just the opposite—they don't have any nunchi, or really much idea about anything.

One of the social functions of nunchi is to preserve harmony in group settings. Those who employ it are indirect and discreet in order to keep the peace. For example, in an office environment, a colleague might say "yes" when they mean "no," knowing that it would be more awkward to disappoint. Having nunchi means knowing that what they really mean is "no," and responding accordingly without ever exposing the lie.

The closest equivalent in the English language is the concept of "emotional intelligence," a pseudo-psychological term that refers to the ability to read your own emotions and those of the people around you accurately and with empathy. Frequently co-opted by the corporate self-help industry, it's a term most often used in the context of an individual's pursuits—how someone can employ it in order to achieve their goals.

By contrast, nunchi is as much about understanding one's status and place in a hierarchy as it is about reading emotional cues. Since as far back as the 16th century, Koreans have employed nunchi to read their oppressors or opponents, and find some advantage. Today's Korean society is very much built on age hierarchy; the status rules and traditions formed over centuries continue to reign. Employment of nunchi assists in the navigation of complex and nuanced interactions between those with status and those without.

Use: The Korean drinking game Nunchi Game is an excellent test of one's nunchi credentials. The first player begins by standing and saying "one." Other players must then use nunchi to sense who's going to continue the game by standing and saying "two," then "three," and so on. If two players stand and say the next number at the same time, they have failed to read the room and so lose the game.

Photograph: Emma Hartvig

How to use scientific skepticism as an antidote to large-scale deception.

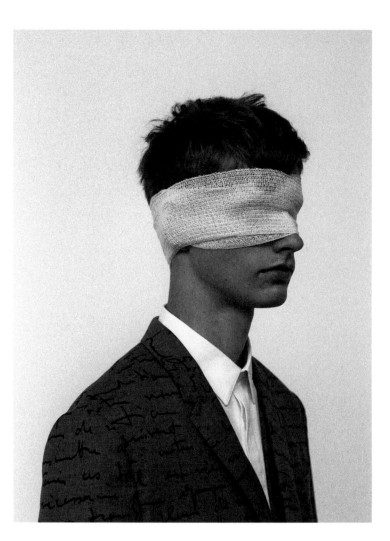

CHARLES BETHEA

Hold the Phony

Carl Sagan was one of the 20th century's most celebrated scientists and is often associated with the 1980s television series *Cosmos*. By the mid-'90s, his reputation had helped the show to amass some 500 million viewers in 60 countries.

A year before his death in 1996, the beloved American cosmologist and author Carl Sagan wrote *The Fine Art of Baloney Detection*—the best 20th-century essay on the subject of bullshit. "In the final tolling," he wrote, "it often turns out that the facts are more comforting than the fantasy."

Citing aspirin commercials, Whole Life Expos, the use of dousing rods to find mineral deposits and "psychic surgeons" to cure all manner of disease, Sagan addresses the "steady rainfall of deception" that moistens modern life. "These," he writes, "are all cases of proved or presumptive baloney. A deception arises, sometimes innocently but collaboratively, sometimes with cynical premeditation. Usually the victim is caught up in a powerful emotion—wonder, fear, greed, grief. Credulous acceptance of baloney can cost you money. . . But it can be much more dangerous than that, and when governments and societies lose the capacity for critical thinking, the results can be catastrophic." Rising sea levels, for instance. Nuclear fallout. Tweeters-in-chief.

Leaning on his like-minded predecessors—including Clement, Hume, Huxley and Paine—Sagan outlines a straightforward guide for separating the scientifically sound wheat from the enticing but ultimately illusory chaff. Though we may not be able to control whether Donald Trump believes in the science proving climate change, it's possible for the rest of us to batten down our mental hatches.

The dos and don'ts of Sagan's tool kit for the aspiring skeptic: *Do* gather facts, engage in debate, seek multiple perspectives, detach emotion, quantify data, control experiments, separate variables. *Don't* attack the person behind an opposing idea, believe in so-called authority, create false dichotomies, speak of slippery slopes, suppress evidence, muddle language, cherry-pick the numbers or deliberately misunderstand them. Seek reason, in essence, and recognize fraud. (It's almost like politicians have confused the dos with the don'ts.)

As it turns out, you need not be a master of transfinite arithmetic to know what your gut has generally confirmed. But hold that gut feeling up to the cold light of reason anyway, for, as Sagan reminds us using the example of the cigarette industry, "Gullibility kills."

Photograph: Fabien Kruszelnicki

RAINS

Drip, drip, drip.

rains.com

Naomi and Lisa hope that Ibeyi's music is timeless: "Sometimes, we have three generations in our audience. We love that." Naomi (left) and Lisa (right) wear a top and dress by Apiece Apart.

Photograph: Amber Mahoney, Styling: Shibon Kennedy, Makeup: Ernani Souza, Hair: Peter Matteliano

Ibeyi

A Yoruba word meaning "twins": Meet sisters
Lisa-Kaindé and Naomi Diaz.

Despite sharing the same background and working together for several years, Lisa-Kaindé Diaz and Naomi Diaz—the twin sisters behind the band Ibeyi—couldn't be more different.

They grew up in Paris, spent time living in London and are of Cuban and Venezuelan descent. They speak French and Spanish when they're together, but sing in English and Yoruba—a Nigerian dialect brought to Cuba through the slave trade. "We were never going to be similar. Why should we be?" says Naomi.

From the get-go, Ibeyi has been a band with global reach. Since releasing a debut album in 2015, they've been touring almost constantly, playing everything from festivals to fashion shows. "I think we've grown up, but I don't think we've changed," says Naomi, reflecting on the whirlwind of their late teens and early 20s.

Naomi's goal is to get crowds dancing. Sitting on top of her cajón—a boxlike percussive instrument—she slaps out the rhythm that drives Ibeyi. Her loyalty is to hip-hop, dancehall and electronica, elements of which she incorporates into production for the band. Lisa, who leads on vocals, is soulful and serene. Her edges feel softer, her presence more grounded.

Yin and yang is the metaphor one might naturally reach for, but the sisters prefer its Yoruba equivalent: Lisa is the daughter of Yemaya, the mothering water goddess, while Naomi is the daughter of Shango, a disruptive spirit of thunder.

One reviewer described the musical output of this collaboration as "doom soul." It's an accurate description of Ibeyi's first album. Weighted by prayers, chants and aching melodic arcs, these early songs were written as the sisters were mourning two deaths: of their father, legendary Buena Vista Social Club percussionist Angá Diaz, and of their older sister, Yanira. "I guess the first album was about us in the past—our father and our sister, us from the ages of 14 to 19," says Lisa. "I don't think we could get much more personal than that."

But doom soul doesn't begin to capture the intention of the band's second release. Driven by Naomi's insistence that the songs should have an "animal energy," the tempo has been turned up and the focus has been flipped inside out: In the place of ghosts, the sisters are singing about the future. "We are obsessed with artists who create something beautiful with their pain, sorrow and scars," explains Lisa. She cites the song "Deathless" as an example of this new outward-looking focus. "At first it was a song about a racist encounter with a policeman that I had when I was 16. But really quickly I realized we wanted to write a song for everybody, for when you feel small and little and people are not treating you well and for three minutes you need to feel large and powerful," she explains. "And I think we needed to hear it, Naomi and I. It's a little resistance anthem."

Perhaps Ibeyi also felt compelled to start making music with a public message because they suddenly realized everyone was watching. In April last year, the sisters were swept up in a rush of celebrity when Beyoncé selected them to star alongside her in the video for *Lemonade,* her visual album, which drew heavily on Yoruba culture in its imagery. It prompted a flush of mainstream interest in the Diaz sisters and their roots. "It's definitely something amazing, that Beyoncé would have been touched by Yoruba culture and would have wanted to work with it," Lisa says of the collaboration.

Shortly after, they opened Chanel's cruise collection show in Havana. Despite having been born in Paris, the sisters lived in the Cuban capital as children and still visit frequently. Did they feel at all uneasy about the arrival of such a huge, high-end brand in the previously isolated country? Lisa says not. "When we learned we were going to open the show we were quite surprised. We thought if they're asking us, French Cubans, to open a Chanel show singing Yoruba then they must really want to respect Cuba," she says. "And seeing how our friends reacted knowing that such an old and amazing fashion house would come to Cuba and share that moment with them was incredible."

It was a striking moment. In the dusky light of early evening, the sisters appeared at the top of the crowd-lined Paseo del Prado in downtown Havana. Chanel had dressed them according to their individual styles—Lisa in a crushed pink dress, Naomi in a silver bomber jacket and flares. Somehow, as in their music, this odd combination worked perfectly. The twins looked toward each other, then out into the crowds, and set off down the runway singing.

EMILY NATHAN

Primary Focus

A colorful art history of red, blue and yellow.

Primary colors can be combined in different ways to produce every other color. Embedded in their absolute simplicity, then, is a latent complexity—a potential for extrapolation and manipulation.

Take, for example, the art of Alexander Rodchenko. In 1921, the pioneering Russian artist joined four of his constructivist movement compatriots in an exhibition in Moscow. Rodchenko was bold, as always, and his contribution to the show was a triptych: *Pure Red Color, Pure Yellow Color* and *Pure Blue Color.* The three canvases—each covered in a primary pigment—were modern art's first non-figurative monochromes. He didn't describe his work as an homage to painting, or frame it as the concentrated essence of all color and thus a celebration of the art form's material genesis. Instead, Rodchenko used the very nature of his chosen colors to explain his intention as the complete opposite: "I reduced painting to its logical conclusion and exhibited three canvases: red, blue and yellow," he said. "I affirmed: it's all over."

It wasn't over, of course. Painting continued and the primaries have persisted—even taking on symbolic resonance and political significance. Around the time that Rodchenko was declaring them to be harbingers of The End, Dutch painters Theo van Doesburg and Piet Mondrian saw in those three hues a utopian vision of universal human harmony. They perceived the primary colors as fundamental to their new cultural movement—De Stijl, or "the style" in Dutch—which was dedicated both to countering the decorative excesses of art deco, the period's dominant aesthetic, and to rebuilding society through art in the devastating aftermath of World War I. Its practitioners emphasized the idea of absolute essentials, favoring reductive abstractions and simple visual elements like geometric forms, often represented in red, yellow and blue. It

was in the most basic things, they suggested through their work, that the world's people could find common ground and come together.

The primaries found their place in the Bauhaus, too. The school's founder, Walter Gropius, widely considered one of the fathers of modernist architecture, believed that the movement should generate designs that were simple, rational and, above all, accessible—again tapping into the clear, communicative power of red, yellow and blue.

Today, they have been seized upon by Bordeaux's Museum of Decorative Arts and Design for its current exhibition, *Oh Couleurs! Design Through the Lens of Color.* Curated by museum director Constance Rubini, the show tackles the historic relationship between objects and color, a dynamic that has been both complex and liberating. "Primary colors are straightforward and direct—that is why they are sometimes chosen to transmit their identification to objects," says Rubini. "The hue then loses its own nature and is instead conflated with its function: the yellow mailboxes in France, or the red telephone booths in England. Sometimes the primary color is pure presence; it then seeks to escape from any predefined symbolic value. It is the color that gives life and energy to objects."

There is perhaps no one who more actively acknowledged the subjective expressionism of color than the German-born American artist, poet and printmaker Josef Albers. From 1963 until his death in 1976, Albers devoted himself to the subject with an all-consuming, methodical attention, exploring the art, physics and psychology of color as a scientific field rather than a theoretical one. "In visual perception, a color is almost never seen as it really is—as it physically is," he wrote in his seminal 1971 text, *The Interaction of Color.* "This fact makes color the most relative medium in art." *Photograph by Michel Bonvin*

French designer Pierre Charpin was selected as Maison&Objet's 2017 Designer of the Year. Between 1998 and 2001, Charpin collaborated with CIRVA (International Glass and Visual Arts Research Center) on experimental projects, including the collection of vases pictured below.

MOLLY MANDELL

Timo Andres

On classical music and cooking.

Last year, having barely dipped his toes into his 30s, musician Timo Andres was nominated for a Pulitzer Prize for *The Blind Banister*—a three-movement composition for the piano inspired by Beethoven. Shortly after, *The New Yorker* called Andres "nothing if not a millennial"—a vague description that offered little insight into the composer's fiercely intelligent character or critically acclaimed career. Here, from his kitchen in Brooklyn, Timo muses on some of the parallels between his creative process and cooking—his favorite pastime.

Would you describe yourself as both a composer and a pianist? I prefer to think of myself simply as a musician. My dad brought an electric keyboard home when I was 6 years old, and I began to play and furiously write down pieces that I created myself. I'm not sure what drove me to write, but the urge to do so has yet to stop. Studying to be a pianist was a big part of my childhood and young adult years. Writing gradually took on equal, and then greater, importance. I was partially attracted to the life of a composer, rather than being strictly a pianist, because there's a lot of competition and conservative politics in the piano world.

How do you name your work? Titles are something that I feel strongly about. I keep a list of words and phrases that I hear and like. It's been going for about 10 years. Sometimes, a phrase on my list will just work for a new piece. Other times, nothing works and I'm forced to come up with something new. I tend to be attracted to the idea of plainspoken titles. Some composers whose work I admire have titles that border on pretentious. I enjoy little phrases that sound almost pedestrian or cliché at first but can hold multiple meanings, especially after listening to the piece.

Do you ever have writer's block? Writer's block is something that I luckily have yet to encounter. It's always hard to start something, and it's inevitable to stumble along the way. Writing is advantageous for my emotional well-being. There were a few months after the [US presidential] election when I wasn't writing anything. The combination of everything that was happening in the world with my lack of creative work caused my self-worth to plummet. When I began to write again, it felt like everything in my life fell back into place. They say it's unhealthy to have your sense of self-worth tied directly to your work, but it's difficult not to in a creative profession.

How do you spend time away from work? It can be hard to shut off, especially if I'm on a deadline or there's a show coming up. It's about constantly finding a balance between being conscientious of what I need to do to maintain that rhythm of work while also remaining sane. That's a difficulty for all freelance artists. I used to spend a lot of time in thrift stores. My coats are all about 40 years old—I don't think I've ever bought one new. It's nice to wonder how many people my coats have kept warm over the years. There's one in particular, a leather jacket that I purchased 10 years ago in Paris. It still reeks of cigarette smoke—the smell will never disappear, but I love it. There's a certain feeling about something that has had a previous life, a history.

I hear that you love to cook. I've been cooking since I was a kid. Cooking for other people, and the process of it, all the chopping, is deeply restorative for me. The lifestyle of a musician is very compatible with cooking projects. These culinary endeavors make for nice breaks in the day.

Do you follow recipes? I buy cookbooks for inspiration, but I find it hard to thoroughly read and stick to a recipe. I'm much more improvisatory. It's like composing—I choose a process, not a recipe. I'll think, "Today is a good braising day," and then I'll go to the store and see what ingredients are best for braising. Starting with a process, rather than having the finished product in mind, is the best approach for any creative endeavor.

"Performance is a part of my musical life that I would never give up," says Timo. The portrait opposite was taken prior to a performance of his concerto *The Blind Banister* with the Cincinnati Symphony Orchestra.

Photograph: Michael Wilson

TRISTAN RUTHERFORD

Personology

Want a new partner who likes ironing and poetry?
Science might help you find one.

It takes a brave character to ask a new partner to take a personality test. But thanks to a study from the Oregon Research Institute, science can accurately predict whether your boyfriend will eat his vegetables or if your girlfriend is into online trolling.

First, you need to corral your crush (or your colleague) to "answer a few fun questions." After 100 queries—you might need to break out the prosecco midway— most run-of-the-mill online personality type tests will tell you which Big Five persona your partner possesses: Openness, Conscientiousness, Extroversion, Agreeableness or Neuroticism.

The general traits for each are obvious. Conscientious characters are methodical and reliable. Neurotics are unstable and tense. But a new in-depth investigation discovered how each personality type performed in 400 mundane activities over several years. The results are eye-opening for employers and new lovers alike.

Conscientious souls, for example, spurned inoffensive activities such as reading and chewing pencils, no doubt seeing them as frivolous pastimes. They would rather, according to the study, be combing their hair or polishing their shoes

instead. Extroverts are far more likely to tell dirty jokes, have tattoos, relax in hot tubs and engage in home decoration. Agreeable types are the pick of the partners: They generally sing in the shower, eat more cookies and are a whiz at housework. Open-minded souls also scored highly, if you're looking for a lover who's more likely to write poems and smoke dope (with one possibly influencing the other).

"A pro dating tip is to avoid neurotics," says British Psychological Society editor Dr. Christian Jarrett, who also studied the Oregon findings. This personality type loses their temper more often and are more likely to poke fun at others. "I hope I'm never in the dating game again, but I can see advantages to thinking about a potential partner's traits (and therefore the activities they will adore or eschew) and how they complement your own."

So what makes someone open-minded or agreeable in the first place? "That's a big question," says Jarrett. "But, in short, about 50 percent is down to genes, and the rest to do with life experiences." The most interesting question might not be the traits we're born with, but what we choose to do with them.

SCRUB UP
by Asher Ross

Few objects are as reliable as a fresh bar of soap. When we stand in our showers and lather our bodies we are doing something that our ancestors have done for more than 4,000 years—though unlike them, we tend to do it alone. The history of public bathing is important to Karen Kim, founder of soapmaker Binu Binu. Kim makes natural soap in the tradition of the *jjimjilbang*—Korean bathhouses that promote intergenerational bonding and simple good health. Unlike the Japanese *onsen* or Turkish *hammam*, the *jjimjilbang* is no place to laze around. One goes there to get clean, plain and simple, perhaps with the vigorous body scrub known as *seshin*. "It's less about luxuriating or pampering, and more simply pragmatic," Kim says. *Kinfolk* contributing editor Leonard Koren, founder of *Wet* magazine and an inspiration to Kim, once noted that it is the *pursuit* of purity, rather than the state of being clean, that gives us our strongest sense of well-being. Kim has followed these desires down to their deepest roots, drawing inspiration from the Korean shamans known as *mudang*. These "magical, powerful women," as Kim calls them, are still working today—performing purification ceremonies, ousting baneful spirits and curing ailments. For them, Kim created a special, detoxifying bar of charcoal and essential oils, a "black monolith with the power to transform."

Left photograph: Daniele Fummo, Styling: Nicola Neri. Right photographs: Pia Winther

Two entrepreneurs create a new platform for contemporary African style and stories.

PIP USHER

OXOSI

Photograph: Amara Nwosu

Nigerian-born, Ghana-based musician Mr Eazi is a fast-rising Afrobeats star. His music has landed him a fan base that includes Lauryn Hill and Travis Scott. He wears a jumpsuit by Chulaap from OXOSI.

"We approached our business with the mind-set that we're out to show the world a more refined version of African creativity," says Kolade Adeyemo, a native of Lagos and the co-founder of luxury online retailer OXOSI. He and his business partner, Akin Adebowal, who was also born in Nigeria before moving to Atlanta as a child, hope that the site's curated selection of pan-African brands will broadcast the continent's fashion scene to an international audience.

The pair—who operated a boutique creative agency together in New York City before they launched OXOSI in 2016 from an office in SoHo—were inspired to tap into what they call "the billion-dollar sleeping giant that is African fashion" after witnessing a wave of demand for African fashion and design in 2011. They point to Afro-modernism—a contemporary creative reinterpretation of images, ideas and institutions—as a positive force in reframing outdated tropes.

"There were designers producing high-quality art, design and fashion, but we didn't see a commercial vehicle that we thought could make it an industry," remembers Akin. So the partners developed their own e-commerce site to serve as a multidisciplinary platform for African creative culture. Boasting a collection of exuberantly patterned suits, eye-catching swimwear and beauty products, OXOSI has offerings from across the continent, from Ghana and Nigeria to Morocco and South Africa. Instead of trying to stock every fledgling fashion designer, the duo approaches retail selection with a more far-reaching vision in mind. They want to define contemporary African fashion on the international stage—a role that comes laden with a responsibility to educate consumers, not only about the fashion industry, but also about the continent and its culture at large.

In that vein, OXOSI has expanded to include videos, photography, a magazine and even a podcast—*ASS* (African Sex Stories). One video series, *Getting Dressed*, follows African creatives as they get ready in the morning. It's simple, intimate and a powerful visual challenge to some of the usual narratives surrounding Africa.

"OXOSI provides an opportunity to learn and connect to Africa in a modern way," Adeyemo explains. "We're building more than a fleeting trend. We're building a legacy that will resonate now and for years to come."

Photograph © 2017 Stephen Flavin, courtesy David Zwirner, New York/London, © Dan Flavin / VISDA.dk

STARTERS

ASHER ROSS

One Plus Two Is Blue

With synesthesia, senses overlap: Letters become colors, colors become sounds, sounds become tastes.

When a young Mary Shelley sat down to describe the first conscious moments of Frankenstein's monster, her imagination flew to synesthesia. "I saw, felt, heard and smelt, at the same time," she wrote, "and it was, indeed, a long time before I learned to distinguish between the operation of my various senses." Jolted awake for the first time, in Shelley's vision, the mind emerges from a primordial unity in which sight and sound are one.

Artists have always been sensitive to hidden links between the senses. Nabokov, for example, claimed grapheme-color synesthesia, a condition he shared with Rimbaud, whose poem *Voyelles* paired the primary colors to the sound of vowels. Both thought that the letter A was black. To some degree, we all rely on cross-sensual metaphors to describe the things that move us. The colors in one painting seem loud, while those in another seem muted. Some people crave black metal; others prefer the blues.

We are used to thinking that these associations are mostly subjective, but a number of scientific studies point to an underlying human palette of color and sound. It has been established, for example, that music in a major key is associated with lighter and brighter colors. Among other findings, a 2015 study in *PLOS ONE* discovered that subjects consistently ascribe violet hues

to music they consider tender. Theories abound for why some of these links go so deep. There may be mechanical commonalities in the way our brains encode visual and auditory information so that pairs of color and sound end up in neighboring bins. An evolutionary explanation holds that co-occurring stimuli—like the blue-green of the ocean and the crashing of waves—might over time contribute to a shared impression.

In audio engineering, basic types of noise take their names from colors. White noise, for example, contains an equal amount of sound at every frequency, just as white light contains all colors. Similar relationships exist for blue noise, brown noise, gray noise and so on.

We've come to think of white noise as background noise—a radio between stations or the whir of the little machine at the therapist's office. It's more accurate, though, to think of it as pure sonic chaos. All sounds at once, with nothing favored. True white noise is theoretical and can only be approximated.

Pink noise also aims to represent the full spectrum of sound, but falls off logarithmically as frequency increases, creating a *whoosh* that is richer in tone and more soothing than that of white noise. Pink noise is designed to imitate the human ear, which perceives sound in octaves. For

the scientifically inclined, this means that the chunk of sound between 40 Hz and 80 Hz contains as much energy as the chunk between 10,000 Hz and 20,000 Hz, even though the latter is a far bigger chunk. This function is known as $1/f$.

While white noise remains theoretical, pink noise is *everywhere*. The beating of the human heart, the rise and fall of ocean tides, the pulsation of light from quasars and data patterns in our DNA have all been shown to demonstrate $1/f$ behavior. Pink noise has been observed in financial markets and in the aggregate forms of popular music and film. Psychologists have shown it to mirror vacillations in our attention spans. If you were to extract and analyze all the curves and wobbles in a picture of a flower, you would likely find the shape of pink noise. The cubists would have loved it. Insomniacs certainly do.

It's tempting to read into the strange ubiquity of pink noise. It has been described as a perfect mathematical balancing point between order and chaos, a type of mean state to which the universe tends. It is calming to discover that a sound custom-made for the human ear lies deep at the heart of so many inhuman things. Perhaps it was already present in the womb. Perhaps our ears themselves were shaped by it. Small wonder, then, that it can help us fall asleep.

MOLLY MANDELL

Arpana Rayamajhi

Between Nepal and New York: A jewelry designer blends her heritage and home.

What constitutes "making it" in New York City? Is it effusive magazine coverage, top-shelf clientele, 50,000-plus Instagram followers, or a spot on *The New York Times'* "30 Under 30" list? For Nepal native Arpana Rayamajhi, accolades from the industry, while certainly welcome, can obscure the difficult realities of being an artist in a city full of artists. After nearly a decade as a New Yorker, however, Arpana has finally hit her stride as a designer and entrepreneur and is ready to admit how much real work she puts into it.

Why did you start making jewelry? When I was in school, shopping in New York was tough. Not only did I have very little money, but everything I could afford— even the most beautiful things— seemed mass-produced and anonymous. Making jewelry came out of my desire to have something unique to wear. My friends, and then their friends, started asking for my jewelry. Eventually, the media picked up on my work and it snowballed from there.

Has living in New York City changed your perspective on Nepal? Coming from a place that has very little and aspiring to live in New York—the capital of materialism and consumerism—I expected to discover something that I had been missing. But no matter where I travel, I find that people are just people—fundamentally the same everywhere. There's no place on the planet, nor will there ever be, that provides the perfect human experience. That said, New York has been important for me. Living here has allowed me to see Nepal from a perspective that's no longer confined to my own experiences and frustrations. Nepal can be a tough place to live, but its beauty, rich history and people are somehow clearer to me at a distance.

And what is it like when you return, as you did recently? I noticed that I wanted to take pictures of things that I would never have before. My friends laughed and accused me of becoming a tourist. People at home in Nepal often believe that life is better abroad. So few of us return talking about the hardships we've faced; it's embarrassing to have moved so far away and then admit that it's a struggle. But living in the United States has been much more difficult than it might appear from the outside. I might be featured in magazines or have a lot of Instagram followers, but that doesn't do justice to the tremendous effort that it takes to succeed in New York. I try to share the tougher realities with my friends back in Nepal, because a lot of people aren't willing to do so.

You've traveled extensively. How do different cultures influence your work? What I'm trying to do by seeing different places and ways of living is examine sensibilities around construction and how people create. In Japan, there's a culture of accepting the strange. Experiencing that part of Japanese culture gave way to more expressions of quirkiness and humor in my work. Mexico gave me an appreciation for color and more specifically, the way that colors can become symbols in themselves. I never appropriate symbols from other cultures but rather try to pick up on different sensibilities and translate them into my work.

Do you have any objects that remind you of Nepal? What little I brought with me from Nepal has no monetary value but a lot of personal worth. I've lost both my parents, so I have my mom's jewelry and my dad's board games, pens and scissors. They're things that I would never have imagined would mean so much, but they do. I've lived in the same house since moving to New York in 2009. In Nepal, it's rare to move much unless you're forced to for financial reasons. In that way, I feel very Nepali. I need a solid base, stability. I don't like constant changes when it comes to my physical space.

Does New York feel like home? When I was young, I came to New York on holiday and immediately knew that it would eventually be my home city. Nepal wasn't big enough for me, and a large city was always an environment that I felt I would thrive in. Growing into myself and determining how I wanted to live, who I wanted to be, was linked to living in a world completely foreign to me. In Nepal, I was constantly wanting. Having very little left me wanting for a lot. Weirdly, living in New York has helped me to pull back on my desire for consumption. When I suddenly had access to anything I could think of, material things and desires stopped equating with happiness. The process of elimination is very important for me, and living in these two very different places allowed me to come to terms with what I don't want in life. Being in New York has been a huge part of my spiritual growth—I really do believe that home is something that you find within yourself.

"Creativity is central to my family," says Arpana, who was born in Kathmandu, Nepal, to parents who were actors and painters. Though she focuses primarily on jewelry design, Arpana has also studied music, painting and sculpture.

Photograph: Leslie Kirchhoff, Styling: Meagan Wilson

"I really do believe that home is something that you find within yourself."

2
Features

LOLA

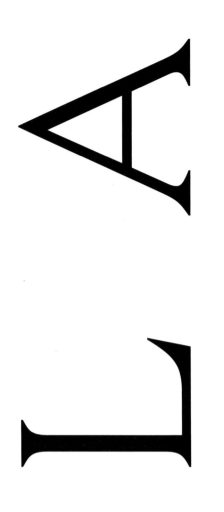
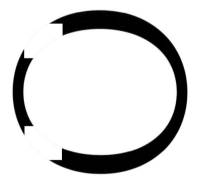
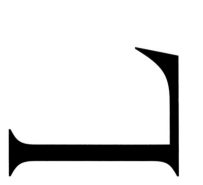

Awkward and ascending: Actor *Lola Kirke* talks to *Pip Usher* about auditions, America and her next act.

Photography by *Katie McCurdy* & Styling by *Susan Winget*

"I often play the subtle, intelligent, awkward babe," says Lola Kirke, slouching in a chair at the home that she shares with her boyfriend in East LA. Run through her current roll call of film credits and you'll realize she's not far off. First, there was Lola's breakout lead role in *Mistress America* as Tracy Fishco, a beret-wearing college freshman. Then there is *AWOL*, a lesbian love story set in a small Pennsylvania town. With her flat, husky voice and melancholy gaze, the 26-year-old actor seems tailor-made to portray the angst-ridden experiences of growing up, falling in love and trying to figure out one's identity in a world that's not always receptive. "I want to play all kinds of people," says Lola. "But maybe that's what I have to contribute to the world right now."

Alongside her aptitude for awkwardness is a worldliness at odds with the naïveté of her on-screen characters. Lola's family left southwest London when she was five years old and moved to New York City. Her father, Simon, was the drummer for rock band Bad

helped me make choices with my life."

Decades later, the implications of Lola's status as the youngest sibling came up while working with a voice teacher to fix her lisp. "She said, 'Did you have to be charming and disarming as a kid?'" Lola remembers, joking that the teacher must have been a psychic medium to get into her head like that. "She told me to say the word 'sister.' Under the guise of making me practice words with 's' in them, she struck at the root of why my lisp existed in the first place."

Although Lola had pursued acting since childhood—"I would go to one audition a year when I was younger and delusionally think that would lead to immediate success"—it wasn't until she graduated from private liberal arts enclave Bard College that acting amped up into a full-time career. She had had a "psychic understanding" that she would work with American filmmaker Noah Baumbach when she first met him, at age 14, at an audition for his film *Margot at the Wedding*. While she wasn't offered that part,

"Someone told me that rejection is protection. I like to believe that I'm wherever I'm meant to be."

Company while her mother, Lorraine, owned a much-adored vintage clothing boutique in Manhattan's West Village. Eldest sister Domino is a musician and doula recently married to *Gossip Girl* star Penn Badgley, while middle child Jemima is a painter and actor most famous for playing wild child Jessa in *Girls*. Cousins in London include Charlotte Olympia, the fashion designer, and Alice Dellal, the model. The family's bohemian credentials are supported by substantial wealth: Lola's maternal grandfather was property tycoon Jack Dellal.

Growing up in a "dramatic and chaotic" household, Lola says much of the mayhem revolved around her older sisters as they battled through their teenage years. (Jemima has spoken candidly about her destructive relationship with drugs and alcohol.) "My 'perfection' or 'goodness' was a reaction to [my sisters'] trouble. I couldn't have existed without it," she shrugs. "But I'm grateful that I got to watch them go through the things that they went through. It

her chance to collaborate with Baumbach finally came a decade later in the shape of screwball comedy *Mistress America*.

"I auditioned eight times for that movie. It was such an intense, long, drawn-out process," she says of the three-month-long tryout. When Noah and his co-creator, actor Greta Gerwig, eventually offered Lola the part of Tracy, her elation was mixed with sheer relief that the auditioning was over. "They had me come for a meeting at DreamWorks. The movie isn't even made by DreamWorks—I think they were probably just trying to seem fancy. We sat at the end of a long table and Noah talked about it for a while until they said, 'We want to make this movie with you,'" she recalls. "I couldn't believe it, but I also felt like... fucking finally."

Lola, who had only had bit parts in two movies before being cast in *Mistress America*, played the lead alongside Gerwig. Lola plays Tracy, an awkward college student struggling to fit into her new life in New York City, while Gerwig

Makeup: Sarah Uslan, Hair: Terri Walker

Lola has several films slated for release in 2017, including *Gemini*, *American Made* and *Untogether* (in which she appears alongside her real-life sister Jemima). Opposite: Lola wears a coat by Creatures of the Wind.

"I'm very good at being told what to do. In fact, I love being told what to do."

plays Brooke, her soon-to-be step-sister. The two have a short-lived friendship—Tracy is entranced by Brooke's frenetic brand of mad-cap charm, her hustler's instincts and the chameleonlike quality in which she relentlessly reinvents herself. But Tracy can also see the charisma that's carried Brooke through life now transmuting into something tragic.

Offscreen, Lola was growing up fast, shooting 17 hours a day, six days a week, for three-and-a-half months. "It was such an intense time for me personally, but also an amazing and confusing and *big* moment in my life, creative-ly and professionally," she says. "I felt a lot of pressure, but it was also incredible to be taken seriously by two people that I really respect."

As we discuss *Mistress America*, Lola is struck with nostalgia as she tries to recall exactly how it all unfolded. ("Oh my God, I hate that I can't remember this exactly as it was," she wails at one point.) For her, this film will for-ever encapsulate a moment in which her life suddenly sped up. In the years since its release, she has moved to Los Angeles, bought her home, signed up for method acting classes and continued to nab leading roles in indie films, as well as in the Amazon series *Mozart in the Jungle*. Along with it has come media hype declaring her to be the next big thing. But Lola, for all her talk of psychic un-derstanding, is a dyed-in-the-wool New Yorker, self-deprecating and slightly tough. She doesn't seem one to get too impressed with her own successes.

"I still feel very lucky to get a job," she says. "It's all about how much money you can make the studio. And if you're not making a studio movie, then it's all about how many eyeballs you can get on an independent film. The empha-sis on money is nauseating, hon-estly. So, as a result, you see a lot of the same faces. But," she con-tinues cheerily, "someone told me that rejection is protection. I like to believe that I'm wherever I'm meant to be."

Her upcoming films look set to further cement her status—*Gemini*, a thriller also starring Zoë Kravitz that was snapped up after its premiere at the South by Southwest film festival, and *Untogether*, which pairs Lola with her sister Jemima. "It's a modern version of *A Streetcar Named Desire*," says Lola of the film's sto-

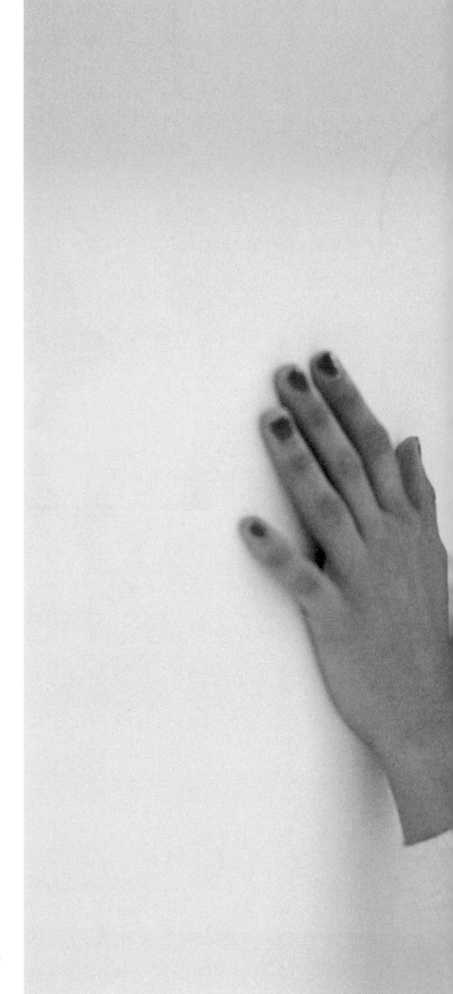

Lola stars alongside Gael García Bernal in *Mozart in the Jungle*, an Amazon web series created by Roman Coppola. The show will return for a fourth season later this year. Right: Lola wears a top by A Détacher.

Above and opposite: Lola wears dresses by Co.

ry line, which follows a woman with extreme writer's block as she moves in with her younger sister and her boyfriend. Lola readily admits that working with a family member was as emotionally strenuous as you would imagine. "It was a lot, and I wish I'd been more open to the alotness of it. It was really difficult at the time," she says. The experience hasn't put her off doing it again: She hopes that she and Jemima will star together in a bona fide theater production of *Streetcar* one day.

Lola is determined to keep seeking out creative risks, even if they prove heavy and hard. It is, she believes, the best way to stop the art from falling out of her craft. "I'm very good at being told what to do. In fact, I love being told what to do. But I realize how utterly uncreative that is and I'd rather not do it anymore. It means taking more risks and making myself more vulnerable," she says. "I want to know how to be the most 'me' that I can be. I ask myself how I can embody my roles as personally as I can."

In *AWOL*, Lola plays Joey, a high school graduate who falls in love with an older, married woman with two kids. It's another coming-of-age story, albeit one set in an economically depressed rural community, and for Lola it offered a vehicle through which to explore her fascination with the many iterations of American identity. "I'm the only one in my family with an American accent, and I've always had a preoccupation with America," she explains.

Recently, she's been depressed by what she's uncovered. As her country reveals new sides to its character, Lola finds herself longing for an America of the past—one that she never knew; one she thinks looked easier and felt simpler. She laments the pervasiveness and artificiality of social media—that what's considered "cool" has shifted away from anti-establishment, countercultural movements and has instead been co-opted by corporate interests. It's a symbolic shift away from

Lola released a four-song EP of country music in fall 2016. Her sister Jemima directed and appeared in a music video for her song *Not Used*. Left: Lola wears a top from SquaresVille.

the values she holds dear. "'Cool' now belongs to the realm of Urban Outfitters or *Nylon*—to corporate empires that prey on what's cool and turn it into an instrument of consumption," she says.

Lola prefers to take a more old-school countercultural stance. This year, she was photographed with armpit hair on the red carpet at the Golden Globes. She had adorned her floral pink ball gown with a pin that read "Fuck Paul Ryan"—a response to the Republican politician's efforts to defund Planned Parenthood. When asked by Elle.com why she'd chosen the accessory, she explained: "As a person with a platform, no matter what size it is, I think it's important to share your views and elevate people who might agree with you, who maybe won't feel like they can have the same voice. My body my choice, your body your choice."

It is in this vein that Lola released a country-inspired EP last fall. As a teenager, she used singing and playing the guitar as an outlet when she was feeling low; last year, in a low bout, she took it up again with more serious-ness. "I love playing guitar, I love playing bass, and just getting to a place with both those instruments where they're starting to feel like part of my body," she says.

This burgeoning side gig has finally led Lola to launch an Instagram account after spurning the platform for years. Not surprisingly, her Instagram shows off her irony-laced brand of wit rather than promoting some heavily filtered lifestyle. "You know you've hit the big time when your concerts are advertised on health food store bulletin boards across Northern California," she writes in one caption underneath an image of a new-age poster for devotional chanting with her face photoshopped on top.

It's late in LA and Lola is starting to yawn. She's been singing all day and her low voice is starting to veer into raspy territory, a sign she needs to rest up for a show in a few days. Before we finish, I ask what have been the most defining moments of her life so far. "No moment is better than another," she replies, "though there were some that I liked more than others."

Lola inherited an innate sense of style from her mother, Lorraine, who owned Geminola—a legendary vintage clothing boutique in Manhattan. Opposite: Lola wears a dress by Co.

"I would go to one audition a year and delusionally think that would lead to immediate success."

Color

A tableau vivant for fall, inspired by the compositions of Piet Mondrian.

Block

Photography by Zoltan Tombor & Styling by Debbie Hseih

Previous page: Alewya wears a dress by Jil Sander and shoes by Mansur Gavriel. Left: She wears a sweater by 3.1 Phillip Lim and a jacket by COS.

Alewya wears a top by Jil Sander Navy, dress by Beaufille and coat by Colovos.

Alewya wears a dress by Nomia, cardigan, coat and trousers by Agnona and sandals by Mansur Gavriel.

Left: Alewya wears trousers by COS and a coat by Proenza Schouler.

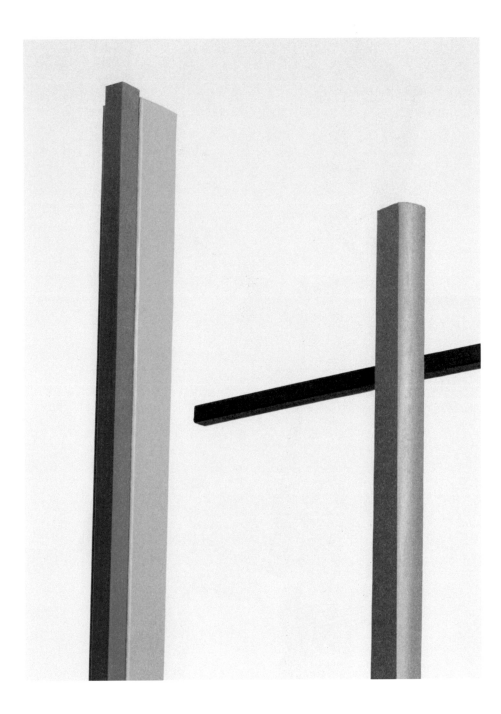

Left: Alewya wears a top and coat by Victoria Beckham.

Left: Alewya wears a jacket, coat, trousers and boots by CALVIN KLEIN 205W39NYC. Right: She wears a coat by Dries Van Noten and trousers by COS.

Alewya wears a dress and shoes by LOEWE.

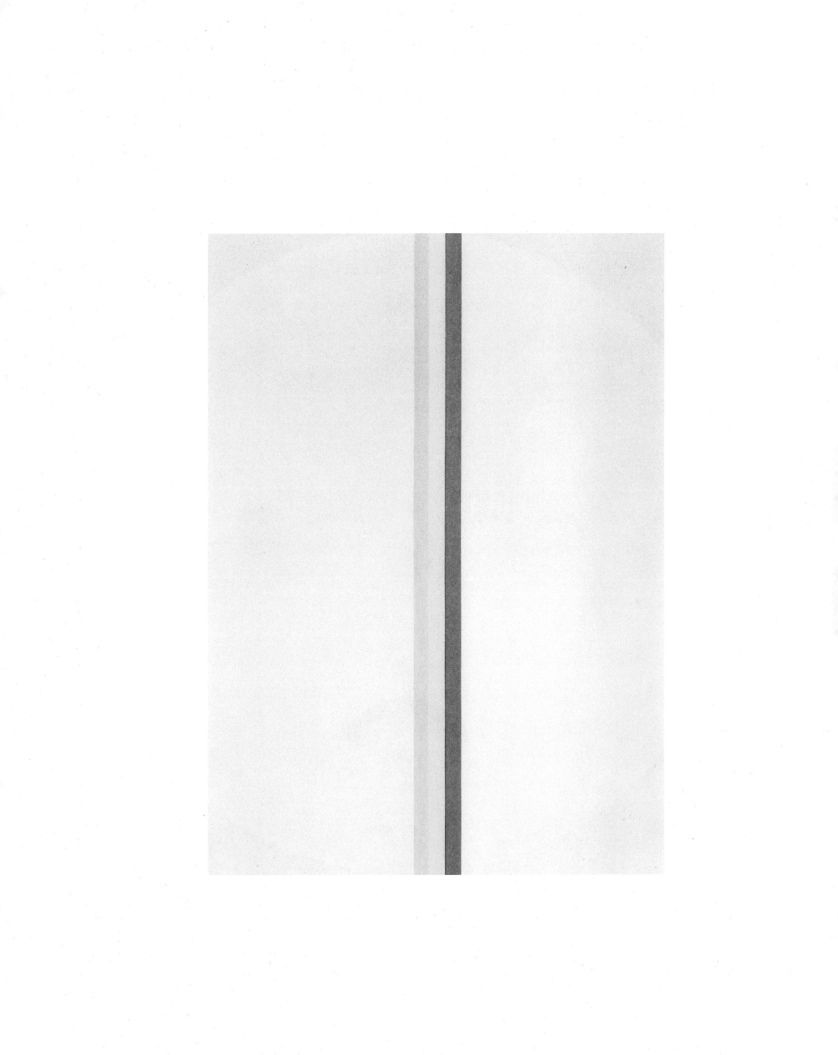

Left: Alewya wears a top by Nomia and jacket and trousers by Tibi.

Facial Recognition

Finding friendly faces in functional objects. Words by *Molly Mandell* & Photography by *Francois Robert*

It's not unusual to see patterns where they don't exist. Think of cloud-formation sheep, that tub of butter that looked like Donald Trump or the image of Jesus that appeared in the bottom of a frying pan. The phenomenon is called pareidolia and is most often associated with seeing faces where they don't belong. "The brain is constantly attempting to interpret the environment, and the result is that it picks up on familiar patterns," explains Nouchine Hadjikhani, a neuroscientist and professor at Harvard University. "It's our mind trying to extract a signal from the noise."

According to Hadjikhani, a predisposition toward finding faces is a product of evolution; humans need other humans to survive, making early facial recognition an evolutionary imperative as a means of avoiding potential danger.

"If you show a newborn baby the general elements of a face—two eyes and a mouth—they will turn toward it more often than the same components placed in a random order. We are born with the capacity to detect a facial configuration."

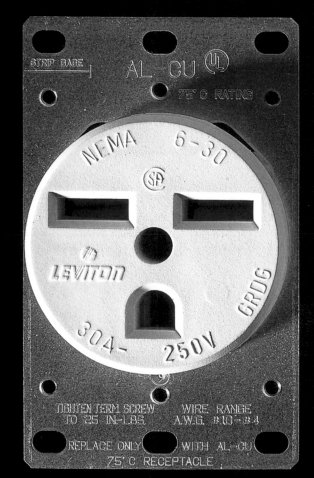

Swiss brothers Francois and Jean Robert both experience pareidolia. Since the late 1970s, they have found and photographed faces on mops, doorknob plates, electrical outlets, power tools and sundry other everyday objects, collecting several book deals along the way. These images are taken from *Faces*, published by Chronicle Books.

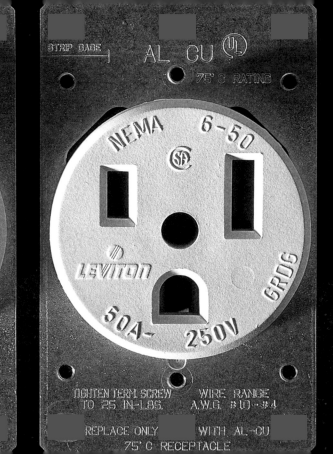

On Narcissism

In Chinese, young people are sometimes referred to as *ken lao zu*—"the generation that eats the old." In Swedish, they are the *curlingbarn*—a name taken from the popular winter sport of curling, in which two sweepers clear a path in front of a puck so that it glides smoothly along the ice. The allusion is an amusing one: Like the puck, young people today have had their paths swept smooth by doting parents.

There are various neologisms used in the English language to describe millennials, most of them negative. They have been branded the "selfie generation," a label that ostensibly references a love of posting pictures online (one recent study suggested that the average millennial will take 25,000 selfies in their lifetime). But the term also conveys a sense of unseemly self-obsession. In the last few years, the term "generation snowflake" has entered the vernacular, too. Coined by *American Psycho* author Bret Easton Ellis, it paints young people as self-obsessed, easily offended and living in a fragile bubble of their own making. As Ellis almost spat when first introducing the jibe: "When did you all become grandmothers…you sniveling little weak-ass narcissists?"

Is Ellis right? Is society collapsing under the collective weight of its own self-regard? A growing number of academics seem to think so. In their 2009 book, *The Narcissism Epidemic*, W. Keith Campbell and Jean Twenge describe narcissism as a social disease that is as real, dangerous and fast-growing as obesity. In *The Narcissist Next Door*, Jeffrey Kluger brands it a "pandemic" among the young.

Speaking on the phone from his home in Georgia, Campbell tells me that after 25 years of studying narcissism he feels the somewhat apocalyptic choice of words used in *The Narcissism Epidemic* was justified. "I think narcissism was much higher than we thought it would be, and it was increasing," he says by way of summary. And his once-niche area of expertise has become a thriving industry: "Fifteen years ago people didn't even know what the word [narcissism] meant. They couldn't pronounce it," he recalls.

What do we mean when we describe a person, or indeed a whole society, as narcissistic? As a clinical diagnosis, Narcissistic Personality Disorder (NPD) was first identified in 1968 and officially recognized in the *Diagnostic and Statistical Manual of Mental Disorders* (DSM)—the clinician's bible—in 1980. Patients who suffer from it generally fall into one of two categories. Grandiose narcissists exhibit the traits we most readily associate with the term in popular culture—they are flamboyant and domineering in their relations with others, insistent on their own brilliance and quick to anger when obstacles are placed in their way. Vulnerable narcissists are less ostentatious—they feel an aching sense of self-importance but manifest it through defensiveness, hostility and extreme interpersonal anxiety.

Kenneth Levy, associate professor of psychology at Penn State University, explains that what unites all pathological narcissists is their near-total disregard for the emotions and achievements of others. "There's this joke that when you tell an idea to a narcissistic person, they'll say, 'That's the stupidest idea I've ever heard…and I thought of it 30 years ago.' They can't let you have it," he says.

NPD is not a common disorder. One review published in 2010 concluded that it affects between one and six percent of the population. But even if we take it at the high estimate of six percent, that figure comes nowhere close to the popular understanding of the prevalence of narcissism as suggested by the use of words like "epidemic" and "pandemic" in the recent literature.

Levy wants to clarify that vanity is not the same as narcissism, a distinction he feels is missing from current discussions. "To the degree that you can care about other people, I wouldn't see that as part of pathological narcissism," he tells me. "There's a reciprocity that you don't see in people who are truly narcissistic."

Harvard professor Elizabeth Lunbeck, who specializes in the history of psychoanalysis, has made it her mission to root out the misuses of

Always remember that you are absolutely unique. Just like everyone else. At a time when Instagram boasts more than 300 million #selfie posts, *Harriet Fitch Little* examines the rise of narcissism, from its roots in psychological science to its more modern application as a derogatory diagnosis for ex-lovers, friends, bosses or presidents. In exploring the difference between self-esteem and self-obsession, the question becomes whether it's narcissism that's on the rise—or empowerment.

narcissism as a term. Her motivation is one of both academic and personal frustration: "Why is it so important to people to condemn the young as a generation of narcissists?" she asks. "I think it's a very old tradition of declaiming on the faults of the young to make the old feel good…but it should be resisted. I think it's damaging."

In her 2014 book, *The Americanization of Narcissism*, Lunbeck lays out a persuasive case for how and when narcissism slipped from the clinical sphere into everyday speech. The term was first used in a diagnostic setting in 1898 by the sexologist Havelock Ellis, who was looking for a word to describe patients in whom excessive self-admiration had resulted in a lack of sexual feeling toward others. He chanced across the obscure myth of Narcissus—a beautiful hunter who fell so in love with his reflection in a pond that he was unable to move from the spot—and named this new sexual pathology after him.

In the early part of the 20th century, narcissism became of increasing interest to psychoanalysts in both Europe and America. Most didn't see it as inherently negative. Instead, they suggested that it was an unfortunate outgrowth of healthy development. Sigmund Freud put this case most famously. In *On Narcissism* (1914), he argued that narcissism was to be desired in childhood—a form of selfishness

necessary to ensure one's survival—but that the child would normally lose their narcissistic personality once they formed meaningful, adult relationships with others. "Whoever loves becomes humble. Those who love have, so to speak, pawned a part of their narcissism," he wrote, a quotation that has resurfaced as a popular inspirational poster in recent years.

Lunbeck says that it wasn't until the 1970s that narcissism became imbued with meaning outside of the clinical sphere. This was a decade of disorienting, tumultuous change in the United States: Mass consumption had become the norm; the nuclear family was losing sway as an ideal; the Vietnam War was turning citizens against the state; liberation movements led by women, African-Americans, indigenous peoples and the LGBTQ+ community were gaining ground.

To critics on the right, and sometimes on the left, these were troubling times. Casting around for a catch-all explanation for the changes, commentators noticed that a certain streak of individualism ran through several of the new phenomena.

In 1976, the American author Tom Wolfe wrote "The 'Me' Decade," a cover story for *New York* magazine in which he branded baby boomers—the cohort born shortly after the Second World War—the "me generation." In doing so he hit out at multiple targets: the woman he

met at a conference who would only talk about her hemorrhoids; Scientology; the popularity of LSD. Feminism and social mobility were all lumped together and largely dismissed. "Often the unconscious desire is nothing more than: let's talk about me," he wrote.

It was a breezy piece whose evisceration of the decade was intended, for the most part, to be comical. But Wolfe's grumble proved a popular one. Three years later, the influential cultural critic Christopher Lasch published a bestselling book, *The Culture of Narcissism*, in which he fleshed out the argument with historical context and psychological terminology.

Lasch argued that the decline of the father as the ultimate authority figure and the increasing dependence of families on outside experts (for example, a growing number of children in therapy) had bred a generation of narcissists. "We demand too much of life, too little of ourselves," he explained.

Like Wolfe, Lasch's targets were somewhat slapdash. He saw communitarian movements of the 1960s as proof of narcissism. He also argued that by distancing themselves from men, lesbians had retreated from intense emotional encounters and that this was likely to make them exceptionally self-involved.

"[For Lasch] everything is exemplary of narcissism—it's sport, it's culture, it's everything," says Lunbeck, sounding frustrated. "What he did so brilliantly was pull this nicely resonant term from Greek mythology out of the clinical realm to describe a situation that he and other critics had been warning about for a while, which is the decline of the American character."

Lasch captured the zeitgeist with his diagnosis of narcissism as a national disease. He was featured on TV, in newspapers and even found favor in the White House: President Jimmy Carter met with the author and used their conversation as inspiration for his famous "national malaise" speech, in which he identified a popular crisis of confidence as the root of many new social ills.

Lunbeck says that it was at around this moment that narcissism slipped its harness and entered the realm of pop psychology. She believes that, in doing so, its meaning was irreparably altered: It shifted from being about how the person felt—anxiety, a pathological sense of superiority, a callous disregard for others—and became about what they did and, more specifically, what they bought. "Lasch and the critics turn narcissism inside out—they tied it to a critique of consumption," she says.

Lunbeck believes that NPD is not on the rise. "The DSM still estimates the prevalence of narcissism at one to six percent of the population, whereas if you read *The Narcissist Epidemic*-type material you'd think everyone is a narcissist," she says. "Clinicians will say they're treating more narcissists now, but they've been saying that for 40 years."

She is keen to point out that there is nothing new about considering the young to be selfish. In fact, the old declaiming on the worthlessness of the young is a hobby that goes back as far as Narcissus himself: Around the same time as the poet Ovid was telling the story of Narcissus in *Metamorphoses*, his compatriot Horace was bemoaning the uselessness of the next generation. "Our sires' age was worse than our grandsires'. We, their sons, are more worthless than they; so in our turn we shall give the world a progeny yet more corrupt," he wrote.

This glass-half-empty tendency is worth bearing in mind, even when considering apparently objective data relating to narcissism. For example, one comparative study in 2008 was widely circulated after it appeared to demonstrate that 9.4 percent of people in their 20s were extreme narcissists, compared with only 3.2 percent of those over 65. But the problem with the study was that while the young people involved were asked to describe their current behavior, the older participants were asked to recall how they had acted in their youth. Perhaps a certain rose-tinted nostalgia had something to do with the extreme disparity that the researchers found.

And yet there is compelling evidence that narcissism is increasing according to some measures. Keith Campbell says that his approach in co-authoring *The Narcissism Epidemic* was to present as much evidence as possible. "We have tried to look at every database we can find and demonstrate that they tell a parallel story," he says.

Some of the studies conducted by Campbell and Twenge are highly unusual. For example, the authors presented data showing a sudden surge in parents giving their children unique names over the last few decades. To Campbell, this was evidence of a growing sense of entitlement. Another study tracked the number of times the word "I" appeared in popular texts compared with "we," and found a sharp rise in the singular and decline in the plural form over time. Again, the authors saw this as evidence of increasing selfishness.

Campbell is constantly on the hunt for more of these idiosyncratic studies: "I tried to look at the number of trophies made in the US and the size of engagement rings but couldn't find the data," he says.

But the most frequently cited evidence for an increase in narcissism comes from a more conventional source: a questionnaire. In 1979, the same year Lasch published *The Narcissism Epidemic*, Robert Raskin and Calvin Hall published a questionnaire called the Narcissistic Personality Inventory (NPI). It was not intended to diagnose pathological narcissism but rather to identify characteristics of sub-clinical narcissism in the general population. The questionnaire, which has been routinely administered on college campuses in the years since, asks participants to consider 40 paired statements and choose the one they feel most closely reflects their personality. For example, the statement "I am essentially a modest person" is paired with "Modesty doesn't become me," with the latter answer pushing the score toward a diagnosis of narcissism.

Studies have consistently shown that NPI scores on college campuses have been increasing since the 1980s. One meta-analysis co-authored by Campbell in 2008 found that between the years 1982 and 2006, students' narcissistic tendencies had increased by an average of two answers (out of 40). Almost

"The old declaiming on the worthlessness of the young is a hobby that goes back as far as Narcissus himself: Around the same time as the poet Ovid was telling the story of Narcissus, his compatriot Horace was bemoaning the uselessness of the next generation."

two-thirds of recent college students scored above the mean 1979-1985 narcissism ranking.

To proponents, this is evidence of young people's growing self-absorption. But critics point out that this particular questionnaire is a faulty tool for analysis. "I think the NPI is not a good measure of narcissism. If you look at it closely a lot of it looks like a healthy measure of self-esteem," says Levy. "I think in some ways it confounds narcissism and healthy self-valuing."

Levy is referring to the fact that the NPI often appears to be making old-fashioned value judgments in determining which answers are narcissistic. Agreeing with the statement "I like to look at my body" will push your score toward the "bad" end of the scale, as will ticking yes to "I like to be complimented."

To critics of the NPI, it is hugely significant that the biggest jump in results across the decades has been among women, who previously scored far lower than their male counterparts on measures of narcissism and now score close to equal. Perhaps, they suggest, it's not narcissism that's on the rise, but rather empowerment.

Lunbeck goes further. She argues that narcissism can actually be a blessing for people who are otherwise disadvantaged in society. She gives the example of a Harvard student interviewed in *The Boston Globe* who had been raised in poverty by an overworked single mother. The student put her success down to the fact that her high school teacher had been insistent that each pupil should "realize the genius in their inner self."

"I think that's speaking to a healthy narcissism," says Lunbeck. "The belief in success often brings success with it. But the popular

conversation doesn't have a way for us to talk about that because narcissism is considered to be all bad."

Lunbeck argues that in the 1970s many of the behaviors that critics labeled as narcissism could be more accurately described as consumerism; the discomfort stemmed from the fact that vanity was no longer restricted to the upper classes.

Wolfe was particularly sniffy on this point: "The new alchemical dream is changing one's personality—remaking, remodeling, elevating, and polishing one's very *self*," he wrote in "The 'Me' Decade." "This had always been an aristocratic luxury."

To Lunbeck, it's an argument that reeks of superiority. "Those who object to the democratization of personhood don't like the fact that anyone can build themselves a house that looks like Versailles."

Lunbeck is not an apologist for narcissism. She sees it as a sort of Goldilocks problem: Too much is a bad thing, but so is too little. What she *is* clear about is that what has happened to the term recently—its relegation to a catch-all diagnosis for bad behavior—has not been conducive to having meaningful conversations. "There are people who are excessively narcissistic. They use people and destroy people. Those are the malignant narcissists," she says. "The problem with calling everything narcissistic, which we do, is it really diminishes the conceptual power of this other construal of narcissism."

But Lunbeck can at least take heart from the fact that several of the more positive characteristics associated with narcissism do appear to

be finding their way into current conversations, albeit with the language somewhat disguised.

Think, for example, of the radical body positivity movement—the swelling tide of primarily young people using social media to push the idea that being beautiful doesn't mean you have to be thin, able-bodied, light-skinned or cisgender.

To its detractors, the movement looks like narcissism in the extreme: Its main currency is selfies, often accompanied by captions that make explicit reference to the fact the poster thinks they're looking great. As one man wrote in an angry Reddit thread: "All this 'love yourself' and 'body positivity' bullshit is turning young women into hopeless egomaniacs."

But there's an important distinction to be made. As Levy explained when he first laid out the parameters of pathological narcissism, it is a disorder premised on manipulation of and competition with others.

Online, people are increasingly doing the exact opposite: Body positivity might begin with selfies, but it's a movement based on mutual support and community-building. As Jes Baker wrote in *Things No One Will Tell Fat Girls*, "There is power in community, and there is power in numbers. If we support each other in our journeys, the sky's the limit."

Call it a positive manifestation of narcissism and even the most radical voices might recoil. The term has simply become too loaded. But the command is the same: Learn to love thy selfie. This—for young people growing up online, as well as those old enough to remember that humblebragging existed before social media—is a good motto by which to live.

O N O
M R M
E S
D I

Words by *Tristan Rutherford* & Photography by *Ricardo Labougle*

The São Paulo home of *Julio Roberto Katinsky* is a living, breathing masterpiece of Brazilian modernism: all curves, concrete and creeping vegetation.

Styling: Leandro Favaloro & Martina Lucatelli

Brazil's modern architecture movement flourished in splendid isolation. While Europe was mired in the Second World War, it became the vogue for Brazilian architects to design their own family homes, then invite clients over for a cup of yerba maté to showcase their style. Many such houses were built on virgin plots of land. There were no neighbors or planning issues to navigate. With labor cheap and concrete on tap, the architects could run riot.

Oscar Niemeyer, the architect who built the country's new capital of Brasília in reinforced concrete, did just that. His Casa das Canoas sums up the era's groovy simplicity. Curvaceous walls bend free-form with a slab of squiggle-shaped concrete sandwiched on top. European and American architects were shocked, revolted and awed in equal measure. In 1949, fellow brutalist João Batista Vilanova Artigas also designed his own home. Modern materials became the star: bare concrete walls, unplastered stone, raw steel and vast panes of glass, all angled into fabulous shapes barely imaginable outside Brazil.

The home designed by Julio Roberto Katinsky in 1972 followed suit. It was his chance to realize insomniac architect dreams and to solve 20th-century problems of security, privacy and searing South American sun with verve and a truckful of concrete.

Guests enter the Katinsky house through the carport. A street gate is locked behind the vehicle, after which visitors cross a threshold into a display case of Brazilian modernism. This urbanist dream is a vision of unfinished stone. Ceilings, struts and a spiral staircase have been poured to order in the São Paulo suburbs. As with so many contemporary Brazilian structures, a concrete jungle gives way to an actual one. Floor-to-ceiling windows overlook a tangled city garden where gunmetal-gray walls are riven by the emerald-green of rainforest trees.

The tropical climate is both friend and foe. Stone trellises play with the sun's rays, so that dappled beams of light reach the upstairs study. The bedroom requires no central heating, but it does need louvered panels that swing outside the giant window frame to allay the midday sun. Back downstairs, the living room ceiling extends into the garden to create a portico of deep shade. The property's cement embrace dispels the fug of the city's shirt-sticking humidity.

How modernism came to Brazil is a tale of the masses, not the few. The 1930s saw rapid urbanization as citizens of many ravaged nations—Syria,

The menagerie of furniture in Katinsky's salon, shown overleaf, features a coffee table by Jorge Zalszupin and a chair by Joaquim Tenreiro, not to mention pieces of the architect's own design.

Greece, Romania, Poland—fled west across the sea. In 1936, Le Corbusier arrived in finer style. The Swiss-French architect flew the Graf Zeppelin's Friedrichshafen to Rio de Janeiro service, which offered five nights of silver service en route. He was in Rio to design the city's landmark Ministry of Education and Health. A 30-year-old Oscar Niemeyer assisted with Le Corbusier's plans to build big, bold, functional and tall. (A decade later the duo would work on the UN headquarters in New York; Niemeyer was the youngest member of the Board of Design.)

In 1938, the Brazilian nation celebrated its 50th birthday. The planet's fifth-largest country needed more ministries, schools, housing blocks and airports. Niemeyer and his equally youthful colleagues turned to Corbusien concepts of cost-effective living space in the sky. They spurned ostentation and adornment: A surging populace was catered to by a deft, rationalist beauty that became a movement in itself. In 1943, New York's Museum of Modern Art displayed its *Brazil Builds* exhibition. As Europeans were building neoclassical leviathans—or destroying those in neighboring countries—Brazil was building an architectural New World.

The movement was furthered when Artigas designed the University of São Paulo's Faculty of Architecture and Urbanism (FAU). The building quite literally turned architecture on its head. Skinny cement legs supported six stories of teaching space, all linked by sloping walkways to encourage collaborative chat. Artigas' spatial curriculum influenced a student that would carry the torch further, both in architecture and as an FAU professor. Paulo Mendes da Rocha, like Niemeyer a winner of the Pritzker Prize, built his own futurist house in 1964. Its concrete columns and cement table no doubt influenced another young colleague at the FAU, Julio Roberto Katinksy.

Katinsky retired from lecturing, designing and writing books in 2002. One of the people to briefly meet this link with the nation's architectural past was Milan-based interior stylist Leandro Favaloro, who staged Katinsky's property for a *Casa Vogue* shoot in 2011. He says, "While living in Brazil I saw hundreds of fabulous homes but this was the best. It had a tropical feeling of the rainforest creeping through the concrete doorframes. You could be in the jungle, not in central São Paulo." Like most Brazilian modernist homes, it had strong, simple and clean lines, yet was near devoid of décor. Favaloro's team had to import their own chairs and design tomes for the shoot.

There's an architectural adage that nothing fades faster than visions of the future. Yet the Katinsky house and its contemporaries have aged well. The movement's buildings look timeless and definitively un-European. In a word, modern.

The curvaceous white armchair (opposite) was designed by Martin Eisler, an Austrian designer who spent much of his life in Brazil.

"Stone trellises play with the sun's rays, so that dappled beams of light reach the upstairs study."

Katinsky designed a cement brise-
soleil to overhang a verdant garden,
offering respite from the searing
São Paulo sun.

Essential

Transportable and transportive: the beauty of literature and its ability to absorb us in different worlds.

Reading

Photography by Ferdinando Scianna

Ferdinando Scianna photographed Italians absorbed in the act of reading—in Milan's Galleria Viittorio Emanuele (left) and tramways (above).

Reading at Rome's Caffè della Pace (above) and the Cloisters of Sant'Ambrogio in Milan (opposite).

3
Food

An interview with *Martha Stewart.*

MARTHA

Words by *Nicola Twilley*

She's been a fashion model, a stockbroker and a convicted felon; she's also a self-made billionaire whose empire extends from McMansions to meal kits. Martha Stewart, or M. Diddy, as she was known in jail, is both an iconic brand and a very funny, very frank woman who is fully aware of her own over-the-top reputation. In the 1990s, she became known as the queen of decoupage and decorative gourds—a woman who was able to maintain a straight face while instructing her audience on the art of massaging dollops of yogurt into terra-cotta pots in order to cultivate the perfect mold-speckled effect. During her five-month stint behind bars for insider trading in 2004-5, she apparently taught her fellow inmates how to make crabapple jelly. But over the past couple of years, Stewart has begun leaning into the parody, poking fun at her own straitlaced persona by partnering with Snoop Dogg to make a comedy cooking show, *Martha & Snoop's Potluck Dinner Party*, on VH1. I called her up just as the show's

Nicola: So he's cooking on the show, but is he cooking off camera, too?

Martha: Oh yes. I taught him how to make pizza and he cooked in his own home and made pizza for three days. He loved it. And now I think it's in his repertoire. He also likes to make breakfast. He makes delicious bacon—he cuts it up into thirds and cooks them until they're like little curls, and they are so tasty. He puts the whole pound in one pan. He sort of cooks homestyle—things that he learned growing up.

Nicola: It sounds as though you guys are pretty tight. Does he text you when he has a cooking emergency or needs some menu inspiration?

Martha: No, not at all. Snoop and I have a professional relationship. I'm sure I live very differently from the way he lives. He lives on a compound—like my compound, I guess, but his is full of people, where mine is full of plants and animals. But we have a very friendly, professional relationship. Each season, I try to

"I have 21 kitchens and I have many more refrigerators than that."

second season wrapped, and before she stepped back into full domestic-goddess mode to film her PBS show, *Martha Bakes*. As she held forth about edibles, juicing and the size of her own head, Stewart peppered her answers with plenty of laughter but also made sure to give detailed instructions on the correct method or measurements for each of the above. If you've ever wondered about the appropriate foodie gift for a hiphop impresario or how to make the perfect scrambled eggs, read on.

Nicola: You've been out in LA filming another season of *Potluck Dinner Party*. How would you say Snoop's culinary skills are coming along?

Martha: We cooked a lot of different kinds of foods again—I was a little bit more complicated in my recipe selection than Snoop. But it was a lot of fun, and I think he actually has developed more interest in food. He likes to eat but he has… um…he has very specific tastes. And he's not so keen on trying new things if they're not familiar.

think of what are the things Snoop needs, and what is my bling compared to his bling. His bling is very fancy clothes, very fancy jewels, cars and stuff like that. And my bling is really fancy things to do with the kitchen. So, as one of my presents to him, I gave him a Big Green Egg and truffle slices that cost $700. And he loves it.

Nicola: And does he give you some bling in return?

Martha: Oh yes. He gave me two packages of marijuana seeds and he gave me a pair of studded Gucci sneakers—crazy sneakers that I had to return because I can't wear studded sneakers. I would kill somebody. I exchanged them for more sensible Gucci shoes. It's just a funny exchange.

Nicola: I promise this is my last Snoop-related question, but, based on his interests, and given the fact that you are an accomplished businesswoman, you can't have failed to notice that there is a huge boom in edibles right now. Are we going to be seeing a line of Martha & Snoop-branded edibles anytime soon?

Martha began modeling in high school and continued while pursuing a degree at Barnard College in New York. Her clients ranged from Clairol to Chanel.

Previous spread: Courtesy Martha Stewart

Photograph: Courtesy Martha Stewart. Overleaf: Susan Wood Richardson

Martha at work in the kitchen of her
Connecticut farmhouse, August 1976.

FOOD

Martha: I don't think so. I don't think it would appeal to a good portion of my demographic. What's interesting to me is that Snoop's gang all aspires to be "bougie." And I was trying to tell him that, to me, being "bougie" sounds so ordinary and they should be aspiring to something other than that. So we got into a big, long discussion about what "bougie" means. I still don't really know what "bougie" is, but it sounds like being bourgeois. And I don't think that's so aspirational. I wouldn't want to be bourgeois in any way. I want to be special.

Nicola: Where do you stand on juicing, which is almost a religion in Los Angeles at this point?

Martha: I drink green juice every single morning that I make from things I grow. I grow vegetables all year-round in a greenhouse. So, right now, I have fresh New Zealand spinach, which is a very watery, very fast-growing spinach that you just pick and pick again. The more you pick it, the more it grows. And I have mint, parsley, coriander and my own carrots. I don't put much sweet in the juice—it's mostly green, with celery. I do celery leaves a lot.

That gets me going every morning—it just really brightens my day. My hair grows really fast, and I'm sure that has to do with the green juice. My daughter just eats the vegetables. But I don't think that's the same thing. I don't think it gives you the jolt that the juice does. At my farm in the morning, everyone is standing in line for my green juice.

Nicola: Any plans to become a juice mogul?

Martha: I don't know. Juice is very personal. I don't like most juices that you buy, because you don't know where the vegetables come from. I came up with an idea that you could freeze the juices and then thaw them in the blender. And they came out very well—I tried it—but it's very expensive to make juice the way I make it, because it takes a lot of spinach to make a glass of juice. But I don't care what anybody says, I'm going to continue drinking it.

Nicola: So, you love your juicer. I've seen from your Instagram feed that you also love your drone. What high-tech kitchen gadgets are you into?

Martha: I've had a sous-vide machine for a long time. I did sous-vide eggs with asparagus for one of the courses at Easter and ev-

Martha flips pancakes for friends while
on holiday in St. Barts in 1980.

Above: Courtesy Martha Stewart. Previous spread: Susan Wood Richardson

erybody loved it. But then we tried to hard-boil the leftover eggs in the sous-vide, and they were horrible—so horrible! They stayed that soft, gelatinous consistency—the whites never got hard.

After I visited Nathan Myhrvold at his wonderful kitchen, I bought a centrifuge. If you juice a pea and put it in the centrifuge, it separates the butter of the pea—the essence of the pea—and you end up with sort of like a pea-green butter. And it's so delicious. You can also do it with carrots—it's incredible what the centrifuge does.

I don't use a microwave generally. I scramble eggs with my cappuccino machine—they make the best scrambled eggs on earth. You should get yourself a San Marco, a real professional one, and you just put two eggs in a Pyrex cup, beat them up a little bit with a fork, add a little salt and a dot of butter and then just turn the steam on. And within 20 seconds you have fluffy, delicious scrambled eggs!

Nicola: You started out catering in the 1980s, which means your career has spanned really big shifts in how Americans think about food. In the '80s and '90s, low-fat was all the rage, and then there was the Atkins trend, and then the Paleo diet. And now sugar is public enemy number one...

Martha: I have never gone on any of those diets. Ever. And I have maintained pretty much the same size my whole life. My waist is bigger than it should be, but the rest of me isn't. My head is also the same size it's been since I was an adult. Did you know your head is supposed to be the same circumference as your waist? Carolina Herrera told me that. Mine is not, unfortunately. Hers is—we measured. Twenty-two and a half inches. Now, when I got married my waist was 19 inches. I have the dress to prove it.

Nicola: Nowadays, we're all supposed to be eating for our microbes as well as ourselves. Are you into fermentation? Do you have a crock of kimchi at home?

Martha: Well, I was brought up on pickles, being Polish. I cannot eat kimchi—it's too strong for me. I don't want to stink of garlic all day long.

Nicola: That's the downside. Fortunately, I'm a freelance writer, so I don't have to interact with people very often.

Martha: You might have to open the door to the UPS man and he would smell it. But I love *oshinko*—it's very similar, without all the garlic and without all the smell. I eat oshinko several times a week. It's my favorite Japanese thing. I learned how to make oshinko from my friend Momoko Sano in Tokyo. Her mother made *the* best oshinko I've ever had. She made it in a plastic tub underneath her sink. You have to turn it every 24 hours or it starts to really rot. I *love* it, and so do my grandchildren. So that's where I get my fermented stuff. Beer is also fermented and wine is fermented and those are both perfectly good, too.

But I've created a menu for myself that's very healthy. I probably eat a little too much sugar, but I eat a very balanced diet, and I will rarely open a can of anything or even a jar of anything other than mustard, or maybe some mayonnaise if I want to make tuna fish or something.

Nicola: How many nights a week would you say you cook dinner?

Martha: Um...not very many. Although, Memorial Day weekend, I cooked breakfast, lunch and dinner for 12 people for three days. So that makes up for about a month. On weekends, I cook breakfast and lunch for everybody on my farm—whoever is hanging around gets fed.

Nicola: You've recently gone into the meal-kit business with Martha & Marley Spoon—is the idea to get people cooking more at home?

Martha: I think it's the future of food, actually. It's a fantastic way to learn how to cook and to experiment with different flavors, cuisines and ingredients. And it is a tremendously clever way to eliminate the waste that goes on in supermarkets.

We're not competing with restaurants, we're competing with the supermarkets. You can go out and try two new restaurants a week with the money you save on not wasting food in your refrigerator. And no shopping!

Nicola: Many people, even if they're not actually cooking, look at food magazines and watch cooking shows as a form of escapism.

Martha: I live the food porn.

Nicola: Exactly. So what's your food porn? What do you look at, to escape?

Martha: Oh, I look at everything. Everything. But especially restaurants. I love going to new restaurants, I love tasting different people's food, the different chefs. I love going to people's homes and seeing what they're cooking and serving.

I talk about food all the time. I'm supposed to be in a meeting for my eighth season of *Martha Bakes* right now. But first, I just want to know one thing: You're writing a book on refrigeration—what's that about?

Nicola: You'll just have to buy it and find out. But, while we're on the subject, how many fridges do you have?

Martha: Well, I have 21 kitchens and I have many more refrigerators than that. In Maine, I have two whole walls of refrigerators from 1925. They've had new motors put in, but they function perfectly. You know, I probably have 50 or 60 refrigerators, personally. I have a lot of refrigerators. Those under-counter refrigerators are the best.

"Did you know your head is supposed to be the same circumference as your waist? Carolina Herrera told me that."

Primal

Natural tones and earthy flavors: Celebrating the deep comfort of some of nature's staples.

Pleasure

Photography by Marsý Hild Þórsdóttir & Styling by Giulia Querenghi

Hair: Cyril Laforet, Makeup: Christopher Kam

Marine wears a top, skirt and coat by Anteprima and a ring by Hermès. Previous spread: She wears a dress by Lemaire.

Left: Marine wears a dress by Edeline Lee. Above: Barrette by Charlotte Chesnais.

Marine wears a top by Dries Van Noten and a bracelet by Ana Khouri.

Above: Marine wears a dress by Lemaire. Right: Bag by JW Anderson.

Marine wears a jumpsuit by Wanda Nylon and shoes by Jacquemus.

Marine wears a top, coat and trousers by Hermès. Cocktail glasses and wine glass by Saint-Louis.

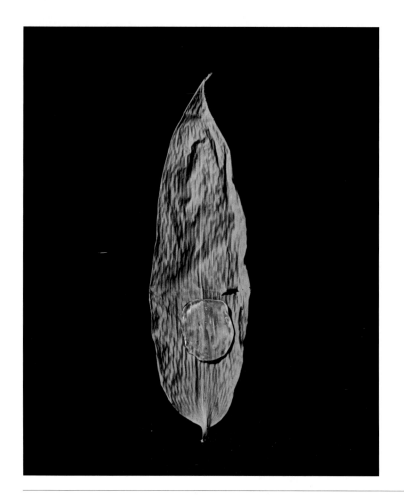

How to Wrap Five Eggs

How to handle even the humblest of objects with care. Words by *Asher Ross* & Photography by *Michikazu Sakai*

Japanese culture has a preference for concealment over grandeur. Take the landscape paintings of the Muromachi period, in which a few shaded lines were often used to signify mountains. How quickly the mind fills in the vast surrounding emptiness, how complete the sense becomes of unseen valleys, of frozen pools with sleeping fish! These were painters who knew how to modulate the power of the hidden, to manipulate its unique command over the imagination. But the concept was also integral to Japanese poetry, architecture and philosophy.

It is a mistake, though, to think these values were limited to high culture. The aesthetic consideration of how something should be revealed suffused all aspects of classical Japanese society, whether in courtship, the layout of a garden or the entrance to a home. It was even applied to the humblest of objects.

There may be no better primer on the subject than Hideyuki Oka's *How to Wrap Five Eggs*. Oka dedicated much of his life to documenting traditional Japanese packaging, a craft he saw disappearing everywhere around him in favor of ersatz mass-production. The book gathers hundreds of photographs of these packages—showing a progression from early utilitarian wrappings (a dried fish bound in straw) to the exquisite work of artisans. We learn to ask, as Oka does, "What is a package if it shows no feeling?"

The book is named after the rice-straw cages that farmers in Yamagata Prefecture once made so that customers could carry their eggs home undamaged. These packages were woven vertically, with each egg resting on top of another. In Oka's telling, the containers served to delineate the five eggs within from all others, infusing them with a sense of purity.

As the craft matured, the process of wrapping became more involved and sophisticated. Consider a gift of *manju*—simple confections filled with sweet bean paste that might be enclosed in segmented drawers within a decorated wooden box. This in turn would be wrapped in a particular type of paper or cloth, chosen in accordance with season or occasion, and folded according to the highly signified *furoshiki* method. Specific meanings were also signified by the bow and the scented elements.

Like eggs, manju are quite common. Yet when they are wrapped in this way they become precious. The giver has not just handed off something sweet—they have created a time-intensive unwrapping process that choreographs a transition of mood. The bow must be undone with one type of movement, the paper or cloth removed with another. Each drawer must be pulled out individually as the sweet smell begins to spread. There is great affection contained in such a gift: The giver anticipates the feelings and sensations of the one who receives it, so that they are properly guided through curiosity, arousal and delight. Only in this way can the manju be tasted in its most cherished state.

The tradition is also innately ecological—too time-intensive for overproduction, too beautiful for thoughtless consumption. It reveals that particular aspect of Japanese culture which, according to philosopher Yuriko Saito, "[blurs] the distinction between the aesthetic and the moral."

But the custom is fading away. The sophistication of Japanese packaging has adapted to today's throw-away culture; now convenience stores are full of products wrapped in plastic leaves, polystyrene "lacquer" boxes and synthetic bamboo containers. While the old techniques do survive, and can still be commissioned at certain shops, they no longer claim their place in daily life.

How to Wrap Five Eggs was first published in Japan in 1965. It captured, in the words of its author Hideyuki Oka, "the utilitarian lineage, a kind of crystallization of the wisdom that comes from everyday life."

FOOD

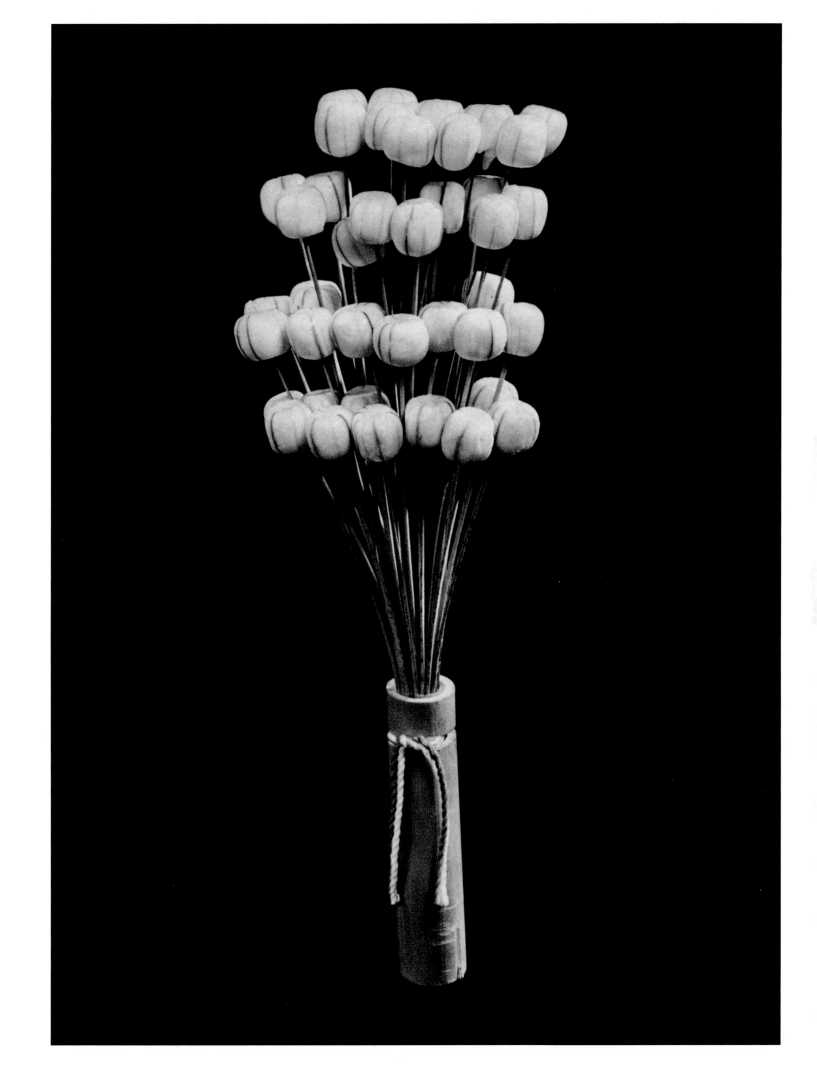

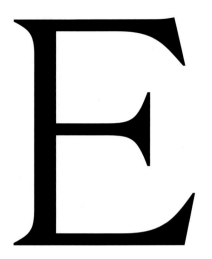

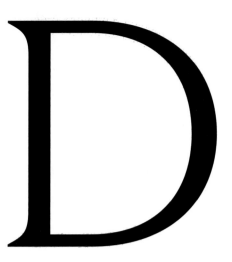

The grande dame of Southern cooking. Words by *Sara Franklin* & Photography by *John T. Hill*

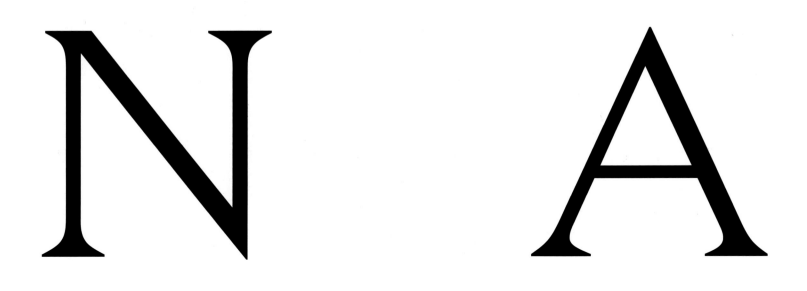

When Edna Lewis died in 2006, she was among the most beloved figures of American food. The author of four cookbooks—the best known being her 1976 memoir-infused *The Taste of Country Cooking*—she earned the praise of the food literati of her era, including Craig Claiborne, M.F.K. Fisher and James Beard. In 2014, Lewis was honored by the United States Postal Service—commemorated on a postage stamp as much for her advocacy of the farm-to-table methods of traditional Southern cooking as for her rejection of the knee-slapping stereotypes of the American South and its food.

Unlike many of her contemporaries, however, Edna Lewis never became a household name. Though she lived well into the dawn of food television and the celebrity chef era, she never had a television show, nor did she peddle her own line of cookware. Perhaps it was due to her unobtrusive demeanor; among those who knew her, she is remembered for her quiet way. More likely, it's the region of her birth, her race and her proximity to one of the most shameful periods in America's past that excluded Lewis from a central role in American culinary history. To grapple with Lewis's life and legacy is to grapple with the South itself.

Lewis was born in Freetown, Virginia, a farming community settled by emancipated slaves that included her grandparents, Chester and Lucinda. Lewis's childhood orbited around food production and preparation. Her family and neighbors worked cooperatively toward self-sufficiency, an achievable goal—save a few staples such as coffee and sugar—in a pre-industrial South.

In *The Taste of Country Cooking*, Lewis chronicled her rural upbringing, taking readers through a year in the farming community with menus and recipes shaped by the particular offerings of each season. She writes of storing hand-churned butter in the cool water that ran beneath the springhouse, picking wild watercress from the streams and walking behind the plow to sow seeds. In the kitchen, where everything was prepared on a wood-burning stove, Lewis was an apprentice to her mother, under whose guidance she learned how to prepare three meals a day, every day. In Lewis's Freetown, cooking was both an essential craft and a prized art, as quotidian as sweeping the floor and also an important outlet for creative expression. It was, too, a way of teaching and preserving cultural heritage; Lewis's menus celebrate Emancipation Day and Juneteenth rather than Thanksgiving.

Lewis's pride in her ties to the African diaspora and her sense of the importance of African-American contributions to both Southern and American culture is the thread that connects her writings and approach to food. As she aged, Lewis grew increasingly intent on correctly replicating the flavors of her youth; she was chasing memories, and

Edna is remembered as "The Grande Dame of Southern Cooking"—the epitaph on her tombstone. Left: Edna bakes a cake for *Vogue* in 1973.

working to preserve the culture of food in Freetown and the particular piece of Southern history that it represented. In Lewis's essay, "What is Southern?," which was published in *Gourmet* two years after her death, she wrote, "The world has changed. We are now faced with picking up the pieces and trying to put them into shape, document them so the present-day young generation can see what southern food was like."

Lewis's father died when she and her siblings were young, leaving her mother to care for a large family through the lean years of the Great Depression. Lewis left Freetown at age 16, later moving to Washington, D.C. and then to New York City. There, she briefly found work in a Brooklyn laundry (famously lasting only three hours at the ironing board before being summarily fired) and later as a seamstress. Her skillful copies of designer frocks and African-inspired dresses drew a following among New York's fashion set, including Marilyn Monroe and Doe Avedon, and she went on to dress the windows of such elegant shops as Bonwit Teller. Immersed in the bohemian scene of postwar New York, she married Steve Kingston, a retired merchant who was active in the communist cause. She also met and befriended an eccentric antiques dealer and entrepreneur named Johnny Nicholson and, in 1949, took the helm of his newly opened East Side venture, Café Nicholson.

At Café Nicholson, Lewis earned praise for her fine preparations of such bistro favorites as roast chicken, mussels in delicate broth, lightly dressed green salads and cheese and chocolate soufflés. The restaurant attracted a tony crowd that included Eleanor Roosevelt, Marlon Brando, Gore Vidal and, notably, Southern writers like Tennessee Williams, Truman Capote and William Faulkner. Using only muscle memory, Lewis prepared biscuits, pan-fried chicken and other comfort foods that reminded them of home.

Lewis left Nicholson in the 1950s and undertook a number of ventures, including running a pheasant farm with her husband and working as a caterer. Eventually she realized her dream of opening her own restaurant in Harlem, a short-lived establishment the name of which, strangely, none of her living family members can recall.

By then she had earned a name for herself, and in 1972, published her first book, *The Edna Lewis Cookbook*, which she co-authored with socialite Evangeline Peterson. A few years later, while laid up with a broken leg, Lewis decided to write another book. Around that time, she was introduced to legendary editor Judith Jones (whose list of culinary authors includes a veritable who's who of modern American food writers including Julia Child, M.F.K. Fisher, James Beard, Claudia Roden and Madhur Jaffrey). It was a working relationship that resulted in the publication of *The Taste of Country Cooking* in 1976, followed by *In Pursuit of Flavor*

in 1988 and *The Gift of Southern Cooking*, a collaboration between Lewis and her protégé and companion, Scott Peacock, in 2003. Meanwhile, she continued to cook professionally, helming the kitchen at such noted restaurants as Fearrington House in North Carolina, Middle Place in South Carolina and Gage and Tollner in Brooklyn.

Posthumous articles and food-world awards have tended to rehash the same hackneyed story of the black farm girl from the South translating her happy, autonomous childhood to the pages of cookbooks and onto the tables of fine-dining restaurants. In 2013, a one-woman show, *Dinner with Edna Lewis*, premiered at the Southern Foodways Alliance annual symposium in Oxford, Mississippi. In it, Lewis is portrayed as a slow-talking, gentle retiree with a thick Southern accent, gone soft around the hips and mired in nostalgia, remembering only her days as a girl in Virginia and then as a chef in the heart of bohemian New York.

"Aunt Edna wasn't like that at all," says Lewis's niece, Nina Williams-Mbengue. "She had *no* Southern accent whatsoever, moved about 90 miles per hour, and talked kind of fast." Williams-Mbengue remembers Lewis as a giggler, with a great sense of humor, but also shy, unassuming and humble. "She was politically astute," Williams-Mbengue remembers. On Sundays, the family watched *Meet the Press* with the television set up on the dining table; no one was permitted to talk while the show was on. "Aunt Edna may have worked all day, but she'd pull a chair up to the TV and listen," Williams-Mbengue recalls of the Watergate era, which coincided with the years in which Lewis was working on the manuscript for *The Taste of Country Cooking*.

Lewis was an utter perfectionist when it came to testing the recipes for her books, throwing away attempts that didn't live up to her memories. Some recipes she only tested when she went back to Virginia to visit her sister Jenny, who lived on a farm not far from where Freetown had been. For others, she obsessively tracked down the freshest, most historically accurate ingredients she could find. She rode the subway from the South Bronx to the newly opened Greenmarket in Union Square, and once requested that her brother FedEx her a squirrel, so that she could refine a squirrel stew recipe. Lewis even had Jenny mail her pot ash to use in various culinary applications, Williams-Mbengue recalls. "Aunt Edna and my mom laughed about that for a long time," she says. "They thought they might get arrested if someone mistook it for dope."

Lewis worked well past the retirement age of most chefs. When she cooked at Gage and Tollner in Brooklyn in the '90s, she would arrive at 7 in the morning and often work until 11 at night. "Other chefs couldn't keep up with her," Williams-Mbengue recalls, "and she was 75 years old."

"To grapple with Lewis's life and legacy is to grapple with the South itself."

"When I was growing up, we ate only what was ripe and fresh at the moment," Edna wrote in *In Pursuit of Flavor*. Opposite, Edna collects pears in Freetown, Virginia.

Edna plays with her niece Nina Williams-Mbengue—daughter of her younger sister Naomi. It was Nina who, at the age of 12, helped Edna to type the manuscript for *The Taste of Country Cooking*.

The Futurist Cookbook

An Italian cookbook that repudiates pasta? In 1932, Filippo Tommaso Marinetti's *La Cucina Futurista* presented an audacious culminating effort to balance Italian life with an era driven by conflict, speed, movement and lightness. Having already liberated poetry, architecture, painting, sculpture, theater and film from their sedative attachments to the past, the "Aeropoets" of futurism (as they called themselves) offered menus that opened the Italian spirit to the "immensely new mechanical world" of the 20th century. The cookbook, published 23 years after the initial *Futurist Manifesto*, ambitiously described theories, scenarios and recipes that constituted "the first human way of eating." However, its renown depended on an even more monumental achievement: removing pasta from the hands, mouths, bellies and kitchens of every Italian.

Pasta, Marinetti explained, "makes people heavy, brutish… skeptical, slow," and unprepared for an era requiring "new and dynamic strengths." Instead of pasta, people needed to be nourished by food "tuned to high speeds" and inspired by "optimism at the table." Pasta was passé. It bred ponderousness and pessimism. It had to go.

So, to make Italian bodies and minds agile, Marinetti and his collaborators proposed a new cuisine that harmonized with life. It vibrated with each sense and resonated with tables, walls, rooms and contexts—an expansive, energetic, strident gastronomy.

The luminous Holy Palate Restaurant in Turin first offered this new cuisine to the world on March 8, 1931. Intuitive Antipasto launched the dinner, and a quick succession of courses followed—Aerofood; Sunshine Soup; Total Rice; Sculpted Meat; Ultravirile; Edible Landscape; Italian Sea, Mediterranean Salad and Chickenfiat. The banquet ended, according to one diner, with two mystery dishes, one only for journalists consisting of sausage, mayonnaise and caramel, and the other, which Marinetti announced as The Excited Pig, involved salami in espresso scented with eau de cologne.

Perhaps the most characteristically futurist dish among these was Aerofood. On a simple plate, a quarter fennel bulb, an olive and a candied kumquat (to be eaten with the right hand) accompanied swatches of sandpaper, red damask and black velvet (to be gently stroked with the left hand). Meanwhile, the sounds of an airplane motor and Bach or Wagner emanated from the kitchen, and "the nimblest and most graceful of the waiters" sprayed cold perfume on the diner's neck. As outlandish and new as this futurist cuisine

might have seemed, it recalled a long tradition in Italy that placed food at the center of comprehensive artworks. The fifth Roman emperor, Nero, famously installed a celestially domed dining room in his golden house. From its ceiling, hidden servants could shower rose petals and mist perfume on diners while they feasted on hare with liver, blood and honey, or dormice stuffed with minced pork, pepper and pine nuts. In *Hypnerotomachia Poliphili*, the Renaissance author Francesco Colonna envisioned a royal banquet that harmonized the food, dishes, tablecloths and servants. In its fifth of seven courses, for example, damsels in red silk place emerald plates on red silk tablecloths among yellow, white and violet flowers; the diners then sample pheasant wings with a sauce of egg yolk, cinnamon and sweetened orange and pomegranate juice.

The fundamental difference between these feasts of the past and the futurist meals, however, is that the "Aerobanquets" appealed in their frugality to many a modern Italian. *The Futurist Cookbook*'s definitive dinners, published in the midst of the Great Depression, offered optimistic food and settings for painters and sculptors, lovers, tourists, bachelors, extremists and every other kind of individual—so long as they first give up their pasta.

Anti-pasta: Remembering the revolutionary recipes of the futurist movement. Words by *Alex Anderson*

Recipes from *The Futurist Cookbook*:

Total Rice

Boiled white rice is arranged like this: one part in the middle of the plate in the form of a hemisphere, another part around the hemisphere in the form of a crown. The moment it is brought to the table pour over the hemisphere a sauce of hot white wine thickened with cornflour and over the crown a sauce of hot beer, egg yolk and Parmesan cheese.

Sculpted Meat

"Sculpted Meat" (a synthetic interpretation of the orchards, gardens, and pastures of Italy) is composed of a large cylindrical rissole of minced veal stuffed with eleven different kinds of cooked vegetables. This cylinder, standing upright in the middle of the plate, is crowned with a thick layer of honey and supported at the bottom by a sausage ring, which rests on three golden spheres of chicken meat.

Aerofood

The diner is served from the right with a plate containing some black olives, fennel hearts and kumquats. From the left he is served with a rectangle made of sandpaper, silk and velvet. The foods must be carried directly to the mouth with the right hand while the left hand lightly and repeatedly strokes the tactile rectangle. In the meantime the waiters spray the napes of the diners' necks with a *conprofumo* of carnations while from the kitchen comes contemporaneously a violent *conrumore* of an aeroplane motor and some *dismusica* by Bach.

Edible Alphabet

From some Bolognese mortadella sausage, cheese, pastry and caramel cut out the letters of the alphabet (thick enough for them to be able to stand upright): each diner gets two, to match the initials of his name; this then resolves which foods are eaten with which.

Ultravirile

On a rectangular plate put some thin slices of calf's tongue, boiled and cut lengthwise. On top of these arrange lengthwise along the axis of the plate two parallel rows of spit-roasted prawns. Between these two rows place the body of a lobster, previously boned and shelled, covered in green zabaglione. At the tail end of the lobster place three halves of a hard-boiled egg, cut lengthwise, so that the yellow rests on the slices of tongue. The front part, however, is crowned with six cockscombs laid out like sectors of a circle, while completing the garnish are two rows of little cylinders composed of a little wheel of lemon, slices of grape and a slice of truffle sprinkled with lobster coral.

White and Black

A one-man-show on the internal walls of the stomach consisting of free-form arabesques of whipped cream sprinkled with lime-tree charcoal. Contra the blackest indigestion. Pro the whitest teeth.

Diabolical Roses

2 eggs, 100 gr. flour, juice of ½ fresh lemon, a tablespoon of olive oil. Mix the ingredients well to form a not too thick batter; pluck the heads off some velvety red roses in full bloom, toss them in, and fry them in boiling oil the same way as with Jerusalem artichokes. Serve very hot. (These roses are ideal for newlyweds to eat at midnight in January especially if they are covered with Mafarka pudding).

Surprise Bananas

Scoop out a cavity in a peeled banana and fill it with chopped chicken meat. Put it on the fire in a buttered pan and gradually add some meat juices. Serve with vegetables.

COOKING

The non-essential cookbooks every chef should have on their shelf.

T H E

B O O K S

T O

Photography by Pia Winther

Words by Harriet Fitch Little

Betty Crocker Recipe Card Library

In 1971, Betty Crocker published its first Recipe Card Library. A complete set, which could be collected piecemeal via coupons or purchased outright, consisted of 648 cards and came filed away in a mustard-yellow box.

Today, these iconic cards—photo on one side, recipe on the other—appeal as much to our sense of humor as to our taste buds. Betty Crocker's recipes date from a time of outlandish culinary innovation: Artificial colors were in, conventional divisions between sweet and savory were most definitely not. If a food item could be suspended in gelatin, frozen, molded or creamed it was, and flamboyantly so.

But in the 1970s, Betty Crocker's Recipe Card Library was a kitchen countertop icon that reflected radical changes in American society. Women were entering the workforce in unprecedented numbers, and domesticity had fallen out of fashion. For cooking to be considered a worthwhile pursuit, it had to be deemed cutting-edge. Processed foods and quick cooking styles such as microwaving were thought of as sophisticated. Perhaps most importantly, the modern woman was a hostess, not a homemaker: The Recipe Card Library placed a disproportionate emphasis on cooking for guests.

Recipe cards were not unique to Betty Crocker. The concept had sprung up alongside women's magazines, which would offer mail-out recipe cards to subscribers to promote consumer loyalty. They grew in ubiquity from the 1930s onward, in line with the exponential popularity of women's titles.

Betty Crocker came to the recipe card trend from the position of canny advertiser. To the surprise of many, the eponymous Betty was never a real person, but rather a friendly face created in the 1920s to front a flour brand. Being imaginary meant that she was uniquely malleable. 1920s Betty was a bouffant housewife who taught women how to bake cakes; 1970s Betty was a socialite and self-professed feminist with an effortless knack for entertaining.

The recipe card format was a smart way of transitioning the Betty Crocker brand toward its modern identity. The cards were aspirational—an affordable sliver of the lifestyle sold by glossy magazines. But they were also evocative of tradition—a descendant of the handwritten recipe cards that had been lovingly passed down within families for centuries.

By the mid-1980s, cookbooks had become easier to mass-produce. Recipe cards faded in popularity and lost their purpose entirely with the advent of the internet. But, almost a half-century on from the publication of Betty Crocker's Recipe Card Library, they are now getting their due as objects of unique futuristic beauty.

In 2015, the surrealist artist Maurizio Cattelan and his frequent collaborator, Pierpaolo Ferrari, styled Betty Crocker recipes for an extravagant front-page photo shoot in *The New York Times Magazine*. It was a madcap celebration of party food: In one image, a woman with shrimp for fingers serves up a radioactive pink terrine; in another, a man stirs his coffee with a hot dog—a wry reference to the 1970s enthusiasm for incorporating hot dogs into pretty much every dish.

For some fans, it is the simplicity of the recipe card format that lends it a contemporary edge. This year, the British photographer Rick Pushinsky has made a collection of cards based on his father's much-loved family recipes. Called Haimisha, the project is a corrective to the plush, expensive cookbooks currently in fashion. "Recipe cards are lightweight and easily shared and, I suppose, sit somewhere between the weightless internet and a heavy cookbook," Pushinsky explains. "They're easily propped up in the kitchen or stuck to the fridge with a magnet and, if made with the right materials, easily wiped clean of Bolognese." Pushinsky adds that he likes that the recipe cards are so evocative. "The format reminds me of my childhood in the '70s and '80s, and I think, for many people, it's very nostalgic," he says. "Perhaps it's time for a comeback?"

PARTY SANDWICH LOAF

8-P   The Betty Crocker Recipe Card Library

TWIRLIN' TURKEY FOR A CROWD

5-H   The Betty Crocker Recipe Card Library

LAMB CHOPS WITH MINTED FRUITS

4-E   The Betty Crocker Recipe Card Library

TANGY TOMATO ASPIC

4-D   The Betty Crocker Recipe Card Library

Les Dîners de Gala

4 filets de daurade
2 oignons
4 carottes
1 brin de thym
2 feuilles de laurier
poivre de cayenne
1 verre de vinaigre blanc de vin
1 grand pot de crème
1 cuillère à café de sucre en poudre
1 chou
2 cuillerées de beurre

64

Filets de daurade confits

Vous avez demandé à votre poissonnier de lever les filets sur deux belles daurades. Dans un plat creux, émincez les oignons, les carottes, posez les filets par-dessus, sel, poivre, le brin de thym, le laurier, versez le verre de vinaigre. Vous laissez ainsi mariner jusqu'au lendemain, l'acidité du vinaigre cuira les filets de poisson.

Le lendemain, égouttez les filets en gardant le vinaigre.

Dans la moitié du pot de crème, délayez le sucre en poudre. Vous nappez les filets de cette préparation.

Émincez les feuilles tendres du chou et jetez-les dans une marmite d'eau bouillante durant dix minutes. Elles sont blanchies, égouttez-les.

Dans une marmite, mettez le beurre et faites-y revenir les oignons et les carottes de la marinade, durant un bon quart d'heure. Lorsqu'ils ont bien pris couleur, ajoutez le chou et couvrez. Tournez à plusieurs reprises et, dix minutes plus tard, ajoutez le vinaigre. Couvrez de nouveau et laissez cuire 1 heure 30 minutes. A ce moment, vous découvrez et s'il reste trop de jus laissez-le évaporer. Vous rectifiez l'assaisonnement, sel et poivre de cayenne. Hors du feu, faites fondre la deuxième cuillerée de beurre et servez le chou chaud avec les filets qui se mangent froids.

65 ILLUSTRÉE PAGE 165

Buisson d'écrevisses aux herbes des Vikings

Pour réaliser ce plat il faut avoir de belles écrevisses de 60 grammes.

Marquez° une cuisson avec un fumet de poisson, du consommé, du vin blanc, vermouth, cognac, thym, sel, poivre, sucre et dill (herbe aromatique).

Faites pocher les écrevisses dans cette cuisson pendant 20 minutes. Laissez refroidir le tout pendant 24 heures et dressez les écrevisses en dôme. Passez la cuisson et servez dans des tasses.

° Marquer : Préparer les aliments avant d'en commencer la cuisson

RECETTE DONNÉE PAR
LA TOUR D'ARGENT

★ ★ ★

65

Rare cookbooks are great fun: the Prohibition dazzle of *Giggle Water*, the raw prestige of an early-edition *Escoffier*. Among the strangest, and rarest was *Les Dîners de Gala*, a grotesquely opulent cookbook penned and illustrated by Salvador Dalí. It was an object whispered about here and there among chefs, a near-myth that few had actually held in their hands.

The book, now reprinted by Taschen, commemorates Dalí's profound love of elaborate eating. It is also a passionate ode to his wife and muse, Gala, whose image haunts the illustrations and with whom Dalí hosted decade after decade of lavish dinner parties. Guests could expect fish served inside slippers, or frogs jumping out from medieval tureens. They dined amid the howling of hired monkeys. These were parties designed to present a living manifestation of the surrealist ideal.

And yet to read through *Les Dîners* is to understand that food was not just another vehicle for Dalí's exhibitionism. His friend Pierre Roumeguere, introducing the book, quotes him as saying, "The sensual intelligence housed in the tabernacle of my palate beckons me to pay the greatest attention to food." The religious allusion is not careless. We are given to understand that for Dalí, the act of eating represented a sacred opportunity for self-realization amid existential crisis. "I know what I eat," he once said, "I know not what I do."

The careful language he uses in the recipes bears this out. Sure, the chapter titles are full of his trademark exotica ("Les Entre-Plats Sodomisés" for meats, "Je Mange GALA" for the aphrodisiac course), but the recipes themselves are lessons in humble, crystal-clear delivery. It is a very sober Dalí who writes, "First of all, let us prepare the slices of the conger eel by removing the skin and the central bone, one by one…" He wants us to experience exactly what he did while consuming his Conger of the Rising Sun. This wild inventiveness alongside careful execution calls to mind his paintings—famously strange, yet everywhere full of technical mastery.

Dalí warns us right away that his recipes are not for the faint of heart: "If you are a disciple of one of those calorie-counters who turn the joys of eating into a form of punishment, close this book at once; it is too lively, too aggressive, and far too impertinent for you." The warning is well-taken. Oasis Leek Pie is harmless enough, but soon we arrive at Larded Meat á la Mode, the Breast of Venus and Toffee with Pine Cones. All 136 recipes are doused in Dalí's surrealism; all are meant for real-world preparation.

Still, the book can be enjoyed without ever melting a pat of butter in a pan. It carries our minds back to an unrestrained era of French cooking, when rich sauces were considered so de rigueur that they are only casually referenced at the end of recipes. A handful of the instructions were provided by the old high-command of Parisian restaurants—La Tour d'Argent, Maxim's, Lasserre—where Dalí regularly held court throughout his life.

And then there are the illustrations—some of them fully-executed paintings. The illustration for the "Soft Watches Half Asleep" chapter features a macabre parade of crayfish topped by deranged human faces. Halved fruits sit beneath them like fascist banners, and beneath those we find a cartoon narrating the attempted murder of a frog. The images are wrapped around each other and presented on a silver platter. What sort of dish is this? Whose appetite could it possibly arouse? Everywhere in the visual elements we find perverse juxtapositions between violence and delight, plentitude and decay—the "coincidence of opposites" that was the elemental component of Dalí's life's work. No opposition delighted him more than that between sustenance and death. To eat well, he once said, is "to die a lot."

Words by Molly Mandell

Foods of The World

"Time-Life Books invites you on a food lover's tour of provincial France," reads an advertisement in a March 1968 issue of *LIFE Magazine.* "You may stop and visit such fascinating places as an open-air market in Gascogne or a charming old inn on the road to Chartres." This "tour" cost only $4.95, plus shipping and handling. After submitting payment by mail, *The Cooking of Provincial France*, written by M.F.K Fisher, would arrive at the buyer's doorstep.

The cookbook adventure series didn't stop in Eure-et-Loir but traveled to remote regions in Italy, China, Russia and the Middle East. The 27 volumes that comprise the *Foods of the World* series are now classic pieces of culinary history, celebrated as much for their illustrious contributors as for their penchant for self-parody.

The bimonthly series started publishing in 1968, at a time in postwar America when a taste for the "exotic"—and in general, an interest in parts of the world outside the confines of the US—was expansive. The series offered an opportunity to learn how to cook delicious international fare while congratulating oneself on one's worldly sophistication.

By September of 1968, the series had 500,000 subscribers. Writing in an issue of *New York* magazine, however, Nora Ephron revealed that, at least to its editors, *Foods of the World* was no more than an inside joke. Author Nika Hazelton worked on the project merely for the money, and M.F.K. Fisher said she wrote *The Cooking*

of Provincial France for the free trip to France.

Regardless, Ephron noted, the cookbooks managed to include "nearly everyone who [was] anyone in the food world"—including Julia Child, Waverly Root and James Beard. Given that the contributors were established food writers, the subscribers didn't seem to care "one whit whether the soufflé on the cover [was] actually a meringue."

Today, the books are collectors' items. Jim Leff, founder of Chowhound, refers to the series as "miraculous," calling its volumes "legendary tomes penned by top reporters pampered with uncommon time, budget and editing." Ruth Reichl, former editor-in-chief of *Gourmet*, says the series "opened up whole new worlds" for her.

Renowned Swedish chef Magnus Nilsson has also read every book in the collection and calls *The Cooking of Scandinavia* "a masterpiece." Nilsson ordered hundreds of books on Scandinavia while writing and photographing *The Nordic Cookbook*, but says that Time-Life's shone for its accuracy and detail.

"It's clear that the author went to Scandinavia. He spent a serious amount of time trying to understand the food culture of the region so that he could offer a thorough explanation for non-Scandinavians," Nilsson says. "It sounds mundane, but think about it— how many books about food are actually made that way? Not many. That's why they still hold up."

A Smörgåsbord Sampler

Eating "Fugu": A Thrill in Every Bite

СЫР

Расскажем о сыре, о его замечательных достоинствах и разнообразнейшем ассортименте, о тончайшем его вкусовом и ароматическом букете.

Различных групп, видов, сортов сыра много. Есть крупные круги сыра весом до 100 кг и совсем маленькие сырки в 30—50 г; есть сыр квадратный, прямоугольный, овальный, круглый, цилиндрический, конусообразный, сыр окрашенный и неокрашенный (т. е. сохранивший естественный цвет), обернутый в ткань, в парафиновую бумагу, и вовсе без обертки; с сухой коркой, со слизистой коркой и совсем без корки; сыр с разнообразной яркой плесенью и без плесени; сыр острый, нежный, ароматный; твердый, мягкий и полумягкий; соленый, сладкий, рассольный; терочный, плавленый, деликатесный сыр в керамике и просто деликатесный.

Сыр в среднем содержит до 32% жира, 26% белка, 2,5 — 3,5% органических солей,

витамины А и группы В, а главное, в процессе созревания сыра его белок становится растворимым и поэтому почти полностью (на 98,5%) усваивается организмом. Эта особенность сыра делает его одним из самых лучших, самых полезных и ценных пищевых продуктов. А то, что он один из вкуснейших пищевых продуктов, об этом знают все.

Процесс созревания обусловливает не только растворимость сырного белка, но сообщает также сыру вкусовой букет и рисунок поверхности его разреза («глазки»). Хорошо созревший, в меру выдержанный сыр дает на разрезе слезу в «глазках».

Некоторые думают, что сырная «слеза» есть прозрачный жир. Это неверно. «Слезы» в сыре — капельки воды, насыщенные солями молока и поваренной солью — и ничем больше. Выступают они и проникают в «глазки» в результате сложных биохимиче-

Words by Molly Mandell

The Book of Tasty and Healthy Food

First published in 1939, *The Book of Tasty and Healthy Food* is a narrative of Soviet culinary history, replete with overflowing caviar tins, mounds of cheese and carefully decorated pastries.

The book is the work of Anastas Ivanovich Mikoyan, an Armenian politician who was appointed as the Soviet People's Commissar of the Food Industry during the 1930s. Upon stepping into his new job, Mikoyan set off for the United States, where he scoured food plants, cafeterias and department stores for inspiration. When he returned to Moscow, he enthusiastically introduced prepackaged *kornfleks*, ketchup and frozen treats not unlike American Klondike bars or Drumstick cones to the Soviet people.

"Food anchored the domestic realities of our totalitarian state, supplying a shimmer of desire to a life that was mostly drab, sometimes absurdly comical, on occasion unbearably tragic, but just as often naively optimistic and joyous," Anya von Bremzen writes in her memoir, *Mastering the Art of Soviet Cooking*. "Food, as one academic has noted, defined how Russians endured the present, imagined the future and connected to their past."

Over time, *The Book of Tasty and Healthy Food* became known simply as *Kniga* or *The Book*. More than eight million copies have been printed and over a dozen different iterations have been released, generally in accordance with Soviet regime changes. Of these, which vary in both physical appearance and political commentary, the 1952 edition is the best known (though it was replaced only one year later with a version absent of any Stalin references). In 2012, an English translation provided those outside the former USSR with an opportunity to attempt *vareniki* (Ukranian dumplings) or *rassolnik* (a Russian soup with pickles).

Despite its many manifestations, the recipes have remained mostly unchanged. Some are modest, like cabbage salads and straightforward soups. Others—suckling pig in aspic with a horseradish sauce—offer a dreamlike vision of the supposed fruits of communism. Noting the importance of variety, the book ignores the USSR's limited supplies and intense rationing: "Not all housewives take the time and effort to make a plan for food preparation in advance. Mostly they only have around 10 or 12 dishes that they alternate throughout the years, and the family receives monotonous meals... Borscht, shchi, cutlets will appear more delicious if they appear on the menu once every ten days, or every week, at most." Seasonal sample menus each consist of a three-course dinner and dessert.

For those who grew up eating *pelmeni* (dumplings) and borscht, the book and its recipes are bathed in nostalgia. Although a piece of propaganda (lavish dinner spreads featuring Champagne and oysters were few and far between), it became, and in many instances remains, a mainstay for residents of the former Eastern Bloc. It is what von Bremzen calls "a totalitarian *Joy of Cooking*—a kitchen bible so cherished, people lugged it with them even as they fled the State that published it."

Day in the Life:
Camille Becerra

As an entrepreneur, a mother, and a chef in a city with over 24,000 restaurants, *Camille Becerra* spends much of her day in and around New York's Nolita neighborhood where, earlier this year, she opened her latest outpost, De Maria. *Asher Ross* meets her for lunch. Photography by *Zoltan Tombor* & Styling by *Debbie Hsieh*

Makeup: Rebecca Alexander

FOOD

While all restaurateurs want to keep their patrons coming back, New York chef Camille Becerra has an additional objective—to immerse each of her diners in the creative power of flavor and by extension, to teach them new ways of cooking and thinking about food. Camille has built her reputation by cutting through the ruthless noise of the New York restaurant scene with ingenious, vibrant dishes that dazzle both the palate and the eye. After heading up the kitchens at the locavore restaurant Navy and the hip Café Henrie, she's now running her own Nolita café, De Maria. She brings to her kitchen sturdy good sense, nourishing care and a devotion to unusual flavor combinations. We spoke at De Maria, where a warm breeze floated in from the Bowery, and where a group of first-time diners insisted on walking over and hugging Camille.

What do you do in the morning before the day starts at De Maria? I wake up, hang out for a little and meditate on the day. I have coffee or a smoothie at home and go straight to work, usually on my bike.

Does your daughter like to spend time at the restaurant? Well, she's a teenager. She's kind of over what her mom does. She grew up around restaurants. But maybe she will drop in one day!

How about you? What was your upbringing like? I grew up just outside the city with a single mom, so I was a latchkey kid, pure and simple. As a child, I was surrounded by a lot of different cultures, and so I became aware of many different types of meaning. My mom would send me to Puerto Rico every year as well, so Puerto Rican culture is very much a part of me.

What's your first happy memory related to food? That would be my aunt. She was an amazing cook and seamstress. She was the one who would bring the family together—she'd stay up all night to prepare the food. It was delicious, always spot-on. On holidays, she'd sit us down after dinner, pull out her maracas and start singing and dancing, shaking her body along with the maracas. She had this capacity to comfort people, to nourish them and to put them at ease. She knew how to truly entertain, to make people laugh and sing. This was her self-expression, and it inspired me.

The social power of food is something that has been important to several of your previous projects. Was it on your mind when you were creating De Maria? It's something that is instilled in me. As a young, naive cook I had a dream that if the whole world knew how to prepare food, it would be a very different place. Many things have changed, but I still think about inspiring people to cook for themselves. It's a small thing, but I feel like if everyone knew how to do it, they'd be healthier. And I see it on Instagram, or through conversations in the restaurant. People try a dish here and it inspires them to create something on their own.

Speaking of Instagram, your following is enormous and very devoted. *The New York Times* wrote an article about how your followers helped you find a new home in Manhattan. What makes you such a good visual storyteller? Do you have a storytelling philosophy? I don't, really. People ask me to mentor them and I don't know what to say. It's about being honest about your life—along with an understanding of composition and light. I just like to share things that I see that are beautifully lit, or have an interesting, natural composition, even if that's a messy surface in my kitchen.

Your food is lauded for its visual elements. All those gorgeous bowls streaked in lovely, vibrant colors. As a chef you have three obligations: You want people to be entertained by the visual elements in your food, of course you want them to appreciate its taste, and finally you want them to feel good after they've eaten it.

The last of these is often missing in haute cuisine—it's easy to leave a nice restaurant feeling bloated. I think part of what excites people about your food is that you use healthy ingredients without compromising your vision. Where did you get your commitment to health? I went through a hippie stage early in my career, like a lot of people do. You become vegetarian, then vegan, and it lasts approximately two or three years and then you find yourself with a burger and a beer. But during that time in my life I studied Ayurvedic and macrobiotic techniques. I still rely on macrobiotic cookery when I'm not feeling 100 percent: lots of steamed elements, sauces with few ingredients—food

"If the whole world knew how to prepare food, I think it would be a very different place."

Camille's interest in food developed long before she became a chef. She spent her young adult years reading cookbooks cover to cover.

The interior design of De Maria was completed by Camille's friends at The MP Shift, a design and branding studio. Her staff wear uniforms designed by Everlane. Here, Camille wears a dress by Zero + Maria Cornejo.

"I think that unforeseen taste combinations can make people think in different ways."

that is very nourishing and very simple. Yet we can't eat like that all the time; we want flavor, we want the engagement of all our senses. So my cooking progressed. But I've always kept with me the idea that food is health, that everything our bodies need comes from food.

That reminds me of your knack for simple yet underutilized ingredients. What have you been working with lately? It doesn't have to be something extravagant. I love jicama, for example, and celery. Certain neglected beans. And radishes! Heavy doses of radish.

What was your design approach while creating De Maria? What did you want the space to feel like? We wanted it to be very light and open, like a restaurant on a plaza. We wanted it to feel like a place where you could come and sit and work for six hours—and people do. I'm from this neighborhood [Nolita] and I knew it presented a choice between very expensive places and tiny affordable places. I wanted to give the neighborhood something open and airy, yet accessible.

You named it after New York's great conceptual artist Walter De Maria. How did that come about? The name arose out of a sort of freak situation. Our turnaround time for opening was incredibly short, and about a month and a half out we were still coming up zero on a name. I knew I wanted something that was femme, but not explicit. We went up to Dia:Beacon, and De Maria's name leapt out at me. I liked his powerful use of very simple elements, his use of simple geometric form, and of nature. And when you know, you know.

What is the relationship between your restaurant's innovative approach to food and its commitment to sustainability? Sustainability is something I care about. What is even more important to me is to create dishes with new combinations that people haven't thought of before. I'm very hard on myself at that stage of the process. I think that unforeseen combinations can make people think in different ways. It's what I look for when I go out to eat, which is seldom. I want to understand the chef's mind.

Camille lives with her daughter and cat in a converted school building on the Lower East Side of Manhattan. She found the property with the help of her Instagram followers.

"Food is health, and everything our bodies need comes from food."

4

Directory

ALEX ANDERSON

Far From Pedestrian

A rambling path: walking the line between civilization and wilderness.

The verb "to saunter" originally referred to idle beggars "who roved about the country... under the pretext of going *à la sainte terre*"—to the Holy Land. Proposing this fanciful etymology in *Walking*, Henry David Thoreau connects hiking to pilgrimage. Like a pilgrimage, hiking may lead to significant destinations, but its value develops in passage over distance. The trail, the material underfoot and essential tokens we carry enlarge the experience, no matter where the path might lead.

The great pilgrimage routes of the Middle Ages, to Mecca, Jerusalem and Santiago de Compostela traversed long distances over difficult terrain. Pilgrims willingly put themselves at the mercy of the trail, accepting its hardships as essential to their pious exertion. Nevertheless, places of comfort and generosity sprung up along the way.

The Abbasids in 8th-century Iraq built fire signal towers on the route between Baghdad and Mecca, so travelers could move at night and avoid the intense daytime heat. Carefully constructed stone cisterns supplied water, and cool caravansaries housed pilgrims and camels for a day or two of rest. In the early 20th century,

the paths disappeared under railways along the same routes. Then pilgrims traveled more easily by train but finished the journey on foot with seven devotional circuits around the Kaaba in Mecca.

Along the routes to Santiago de Compostela, stone-paved paths connected villages and towns, which vied to attract pilgrims to stop and venerate their precious relics—ribs, feet and hands of saints, or fragments of the True Cross. Churches advertised these with high pinnacles and accommodated moving crowds in shadowed side aisles and vaulted ambulatories. Each small village provided water to passing travelers; the fountains themselves—like the small stone "fountain of denial" in Zariquiegui—became reminders of the pilgrims' calling as they continued westward.

In the US, secular pilgrimages to the forests replaced these religious devotions. Painters of the Hudson River School venerated the trails west and the prospects they offered. Inspired by their sublime landscapes, groups of outdoor adventurers financed and built paths into the hills and mountains. The 2,174-mile Appalachian Trail and 2,658-mile Pacific Crest Trail are the grandest of

these, but volunteers and Depression-era laborers of the Civilian Conservation Corps (CCC) built countless more miles of trails. Many of these adhere to the principles of landscape designers like Andrew Jackson Downing, who advised that paths should respond to "the genius of the place... being rough where the latter is wild and picturesque... and more polished as the surrounding objects show evidences of culture and high keeping." The best paths blend the human and the natural: Stone and timber are gathered nearby, formed onsite and assembled by hand.

The path to Lucifer Falls in upstate New York, completed by the CCC in 1942, is an especially fine example. It negotiates cliffs along fast-running Enfield Creek and native schist forms broad steps, culverts, bridges and knee walls wide enough to sit on. These wind under maples, oaks and birches. Ferns grow in the rough joints between stone courses. As the gorge narrows, hikers zigzag breathlessly in the mist under overhanging rocks toward a mossy low-arched bridge. Natural plates in the riverbed follow a similar jagged course; its cascade carries the view back down the valley.

Whether the journey is to a religious site or along the Appalachian trail, special equipment accompanies the travelers. Early caravans to Mecca carried the kiswa, a richly embroidered shroud to cover and glorify the Kaaba. Pilgrims to Santiago de Compostela identified themselves with a cockleshell, a symbol of St. James that was honored with food and lodging at castles, churches and monasteries along the route.

Eighteenth-century saunterers used a curious piece of trail equipment called a Claude glass. Encountering a particularly fine prospect they would pull out this framed, convex mirror, turn away from the view, and take it in again, slightly distorted and hazed as if in a misty landscape painting. These days, booted hikers do much the same, slipping a cell phone from a pack and turning to capture glorious self-portraits against a horizon.

Our carefully laid paths connect the rolling and jagged landscapes as they conduct sauntering feet and tired bodies of pilgrims and hikers along the land. Their greatest value, one might say, is that they carry our spirits higher over the distances.

Photograph © Ferdinando Scianna/Magnum Photos/Ritzau

Walking along a well-trodden path can provide serenity—and room to think. Walking has been central to the work of thinkers like Kant, Nietzsche, Rimbaud and Rousseau.

CHARLES SHAFAIEH

Cult Rooms

Living off the grid: the private home of artist
Jean-Pierre Raynaud.

In 1969, when construction began on artist Jean-Pierre Raynaud's future home in La Celle-Saint-Cloud, about 10 miles west of Paris, he was unaware that the building would obsess him for 23 years. Its design was unremarkable, but for Raynaud, the structure assumed significance because he would share it with his wife. He believed that living there together would "concretize [their] alliance." A year later, the couple divorced. For Raynaud, the moment was apocalyptic. He could no longer experience the world in the same way, and the home that had originally been intended for two would need to transform along with him.

Around this time, Raynaud built a table for a Parisian antique dealer that he covered with square white tiles measuring fifteen centimeters on each side and joined by five millimeters of black grout. The tiles' radiance and symmetry entranced him, and when he came across a leftover supply, he began installing them in his living room. They soon took over the entire house: floors, ceilings, walls, even furniture.

This habitable *Gesamtkunstwerk* opened to the public in 1974, allowing others to experience what must have felt like a hermetically sealed chamber. The house was a reflection of Raynaud's fascination with medicine and a three-dimensional nod to Mondrian. He admired the Dutch painter for seeing humanity's move "toward a more incarceral, institutional world," which Raynaud expressed through the tiles' evocation of prisons, hospitals and clinics. In 1988, he took this symbolism to the extreme, closing the site to everyone but himself. He felt it had become a piece of "perfect, frozen architecture." Five years later, he destroyed it.

The empty grids are totemic and bewildering even when observed in photographs. Their consistency makes the rooms endlessly interchangeable. A tabula rasa, they invite open-ended interpretation rather than imposing meaning. Raynaud may have understood this too: He called one room *"salle sans nom"* (room without a name), as if part of him knew that this space could never be entirely sealed.

The South African artist opens a new space in which failure is fostered.

CHARLES SHAFAIEH

William Kentridge

Failure is welcomed and doubt encouraged at The Centre for the Less Good Idea, William Kentridge's new interdisciplinary arts incubator in Johannesburg. For its inaugural season, artists, poets, digital designers, dancers, actors, and even boxers came together, in Kentridge's words, "to see the meaning made in the process of making" rather than focus entirely on any predetermined goals. This mission is characteristic of the South African artist, whose work—including charcoal drawings, stop-motion animation films, sculpture, opera and theater productions—is an open-ended accumulation of objects, people and ideas. This endless accumulation connects to his unwillingness to suppress the absurd, which he discusses here along with failure and the absence inside artists that inspires them to create.

What drives your suspicion of clarity? It's a matter of taking the category of the absurd seriously—saying it isn't just about the stupid or the joke—and demonstrating what it is to follow through with something that has a fundamental illogic to it. Apartheid in South Africa could be described as a system followed to its nth degree but based on fundamental illogic. It gave me the belief that the absurd was an accurate way of describing the world and, in some ways, is a form of naturalism. Working randomly, provisionally, and with doubt are techniques of the studio, but they have wider implications outside.

"To be an artist is to fail, as no others dare fail, that failure is his world and the shrink from it desertion," Beckett wrote. Biographies, you've said, could be written about being rescued from one's failures. If we must fail, what can help us persevere? It's easy to talk about failure after you've come through the other end, when failures can be seen simply as stepping stones. At the time, all failure needs to be felt as deep failure. It's extremely painful—a kind of annihilation of the self—but you somehow have to pick yourself up and find justification for it. This is very often dependent on outside circumstances: the support of a partner or friends; parental interests; particular things you've read that give you courage. These engines help one get through failure into something different.

Does private art—meant only for its creator—exist? For me, it seems kind of inconceivable. Making art has to do with taking something from inside yourself and changing something in the world, whether it's the blank sheet of paper that now has writing on it or the clay that's changed its shape. It's about the insufficiency of the self. If you are enough in yourself, there'd be no need to leave outside traces to prove you exist Being an artist addresses a fundamental sense of incompletion. So, art that is entirely private is possible only in so far as you split yourself already, into the viewer and the maker—in which case you're still demanding there is an external viewer.

How necessary to life is erasure, such as forgetting? There's a scientific debate about black holes: whether, if an encyclopedia is dropped into one, everything is lost forever or every keystroke is held and exists as a string vibrating at the edge of the event horizon. It's really more of a psychological debate between people who need to feel the presence of a soul—something to continue, something that holds everything—and those who say, "let it pass" and have no hope for further transcendence. One of the terrors of the digital age is that nothing is lost.

The past is never fully removed in your work, especially your charcoal drawings and films in which the charcoal erasures are incomplete and visible as erasures. Would you consider yourself against minimalism? Anti-Zen would be my mantra, if I had to have one. The peripheral thinking that peripheral vision gives us is an important way of making sense of the world. It's obviously easier to pare down things and just have the main idea. But sometimes the mess at the edges—yesterday's newspaper, not just the perfect Ming vase—is the connection we need to see how things that seem fragmentary and at the edge are actually fundamental to our construction.

Opposite: *Head (Brushwork I)*, Laser-cut steel painted with acrylic based paint, 2015.

Photograph: Courtesy of Marian Goodman Gallery and William Kentridge.

To stay together, fight better.

ASHER ROSS

The Good Fight

Conflict is a part of most romantic relationships—and in a certain sense, if there are no arguments there may not be enough at stake. Yet certain types of chronic arguing can be a sign of abuse or dysfunction. Some psychologists point to a qualitative difference between conflict driven by disagreement and that driven by contempt. Psychologist John Gottman popularized this distinction with his suggestion that contempt is the greatest single predictor of a failed marriage, and is "poisonous to a relationship because it conveys disgust."

So how do we learn to fight in a constructive way? We can strive to remember that regardless of an argument's apparent subject, there are often undercurrents in which both parties are trying to defend essential parts of themselves. Dr. Gottman describes these undercurrents in his book *Principia Amoris.*

"They can't reach a compromise or even an emotional understanding of one another's position because they're not really just talking about finances (for example). They are talking about really important philosophical concepts like freedom or power or love, or what it means to be who they are, their family or cultural legacy. They are really arguing about their belief systems and why it truly matters. That's why people can't yield easily, unless that is understood and honored."

Which is to say that our partners are sometimes fighting to preserve those aspects of themselves that attracted us to them in the first place. It's hard to remember this in the heat of the moment: Our desire for comeuppance often leads us to go on fighting even after concessions have been made. But good partners learn to seize on those small instances when concern, humor, even affection for the other person revive. Cultivate an appreciation for these moments and they may come more often.

THE JOY OF SOLITUDE
by Asher Ross

Science has lots of scary things to say about the negative effects of loneliness, but solitude, and the spiritual renewal it can bring, are an essential part of a healthy human experience. After all, there are certain parts of our minds that belong to us and us alone. Poet William Carlos Williams, describing his private life within the family home, wrote, "I am lonely, lonely. / I was born to be lonely, / I am best so!" Psychologist Terri Orbuch, who has conducted a large-scale study of hundreds of relationships since 1986, cites lack of time spent alone as a major cause of relationship unhappiness—she notes that it's a more common problem than sexual dissatisfaction. Solitude allows us to confirm that our relationship has not come at the cost of truth, that our private perceptions need not be subsumed by compromise and that the love we set out from will be waiting for us on our return, to be felt anew.

Left photograph: Chris Schoonover & Jonathan Schoonover. Right photograph: Chris Schoonover

MICAH NATHAN

Moon Museum

What do a penis, Mickey Mouse and an ouroboric knot have in common?

Photograph © René Burri/Magnum Photos/Ritzau

Astronauts are said to have left more than 70 objects behind on the moon, including two golf balls, several photographs and a memorial to fallen cosmonauts.

In 1969, American sculptor Forrest Myers asked Andy Warhol, Claes Oldenburg, David Novros, Robert Rauschenberg and John Chamberlain to draw a little something for the Apollo 12 mission. Their sketches would be shrunk and etched in tantalum nitride onto a 1.9-by-1.3-centimeter ceramic chip, which would then be smuggled aboard the Apollo 12 lunar module and left on the moon. Myers' mission, according to mostly verified rumor (and a cryptic telegram), was a success.

The convergence of sci-fi and modern art had reached its apotheosis: the moon as an ideal gallery—a floating rock the color of bone ash, with an atmosphere so thin that distant mountains are as clear to the eye as the nearest stone—and a ceramic chip as the perfect canvas. The result is a cosmic cave drawing: futuristic, primordial and carved with sharpened sticks. It makes Kubrick's flying bone seem rather on the nose.

Warhol drew a penis; Rauschenberg, a tilting line; Novros created something resembling a photo negative of a Mondrian fragment. Myers added an ouroboric knot and Oldenburg—perhaps intentionally, or else accidentally—mirrored Warhol's puerile sketch with a Mickey Mouse parody. Chamberlain's labyrinth provides balance: a circuit board containing mechanized elements of the five preceding drawings. Either the artists referred to one another's work, or Myers arranged the order to make it seem so. Whatever the truth, the effect is extraordinary: a history of art distilled onto a small ceramic chip.

It's a literary feast of a puzzle. Bon appétit!

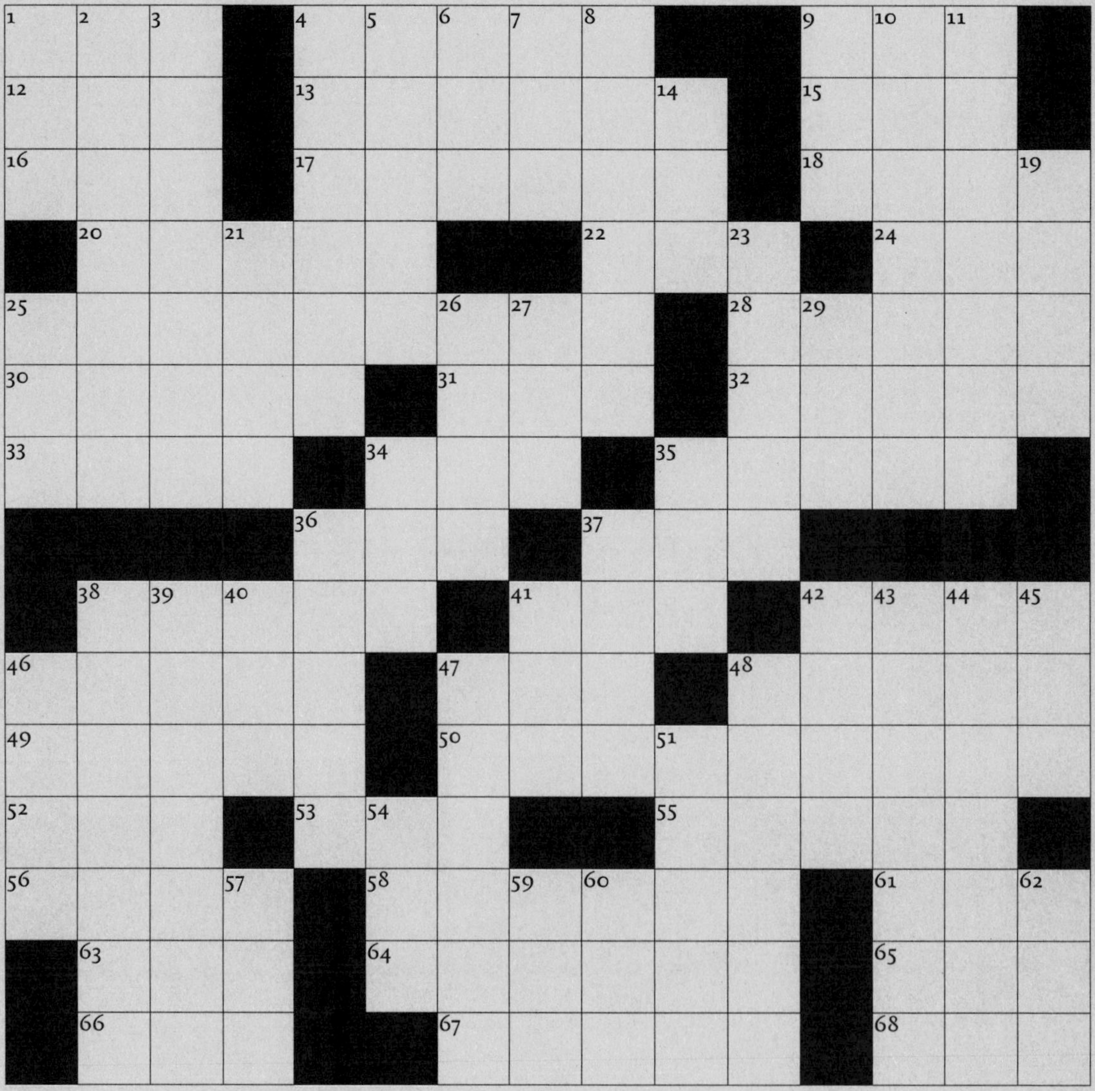

<!-- crossword grid -->

MOLLY YOUNG

Crossword

ACROSS

1. Not on
4. Food doled out to orphans in Dickens's "Oliver Twist"
9. Prohibit
12. Architect Mies van ___Rohe
13. Merited
15. The night before Christmas
16. Dr. of hip-hop
17. Age for a nonagenarian
18. Medical professionals, for short
20. Leases
22. The Mad Hatter's tipple of choice in "Alice's Adventures in Wonderland"
24. Equipment for a pool game
25. Memory-inducing morsel in Marcel Proust's "In Search of Lost Time"
28. Fluff up, as hair
30. Ascended
31. Sedan or convertible
32. The longest continuous mountain range on earth
33. Darkens
34. Half of a bikini

35. Deluge
36. Cookware to bake brownies in
37. Protein-rich dish often served with rotis or chapati
38. Fragment
41. Rowboat propeller
42. Old Hollywood actress ___ Hayworth
46. Pains
47. "Cogito ergo ___"
48. Restrict
49. American high school dances
50. Exotic fruit sampled by the heroine of "Madame Bovary"
52. Church seat
53. One element of Freud's model of the human psyche
55. Out on the ocean
56. Sultry-voiced chanteuse from Nigeria
58. Not out on the town, say
61. Month with "Fools' Day," for short
63. First name for two of the Spice Girls
64. Ranges
65. American govt. spy agency

66. ___ Lanka
67. Ingredient in beer and bread
68. Beanie or fedora

_____

DOWN

1. Quirky
2. Italian automobile brand whose logo features a stallion
3. 2010 novel by J.Franzen
4. Mild
5. Rear, as children
6. Cousin of a samovar
7. Suffix for many chemicals
8. Correspondence (pre-email)
9. Sleeping spot
10. Comfort food in Sylvia Plath's "The Bell Jar"
11. Removed from a legal case
14. Color, as in Easter eggs
19. Observes
21. Loch ___ (Scottish lake)
23. In the least
25. Angry
26. Image on a computer screen
27. Conk out for a bit

29. "Taking Tiger Mountain" artist
34. Faucet
35. Distant
36. So yesterday
37. 2017 album, Kendrick Lamar
38. Shrieks
39. Savory bowlful enjoyed by Ishmael in "Moby-Dick"
40. Band fronted by M. Stipe
41. French assent
42. Shreds
43. Accuse an official of misconduct
44. Farm-raised fish thats been eaten since Biblical times
45. Gobbled
46. Lyft and Instagram, to name two
47. Acne-ridden?
48. Newest
51. ____ lounge chair produced by Herman Miller
54. Fuel
57. Biblical judge
59. Gardening tool
60. Egg cells
62. Tattletale

EDITORIAL BOARD

Jonas Bjerre-Poulsen

Kinfolk's contributing editor *Jonas Bjerre-Poulsen* is co-founder of Copenhagen-based architecture and design firm Norm Architects. Usually tasked with providing aesthetic counsel to an impressive list of clients, here he offers some friendly guidance to his younger self.

Illustration: Chidy Wayne

What piece of advice would you give a younger version of yourself?
I would love to go back in time and tell myself not to be so insecure and shy, to care less about what others think of me. I'd tell myself to act more freely and throw away all the inhibitions that I had. There are very few things in life that I regret, and I've always pursued my dreams. But looking back, there were so many people that I could have met, so many interesting conversations that I could have had. Respecting other people and being sensitive to your surroundings is a good thing, but it shouldn't limit the way you act, talk or feel. I guess it's natural to become more self-confident with age, and doing so allowed me to unleash potential within myself that was inhibited before.

W I N T E R 2 0 1 8

Stockists

3.1 PHILLIP LIM
31philliplim.com

ACNE STUDIOS
acnestudios.com

A DÉTACHER
adetacher.com

ANA KHOURI
anakhouri.com

ANTEPRIMA
anteprima.com

APIECE APART
apieceapart.com

APUNTOB
apuntob.com

ARPANA RAYAMAJHI
arpanarayamajhi.com

BEAUFILLE
beaufille.com

BINU BINU
binu-binu.com

BUILDING BLOCK
building--block.com

CALVIN KLEIN 205W39NYC
calvinklein.com

CÉLINE
celine.com

CHARLOTTE CHESNAIS
charlottechesnais.com

CHLOÉ
chloe.com

CO
co-collections.com

COCLICO
coclico.com

COLOVOS
colovos.com

COS
cosstores.com

CREATURES OF THE WIND
creaturesofthewind.com

DRIES VAN NOTEN
driesvannoten.com

EDELINE LEE
edelinelee.com

ERIK JØRGENSEN
erik-joergensen.com

FLOYD DETROIT
floyddetroit.com

HENRIK VIBSKOV
henrikvibskov.com

HERMÈS
hermes.com

IITTALA
iittala.com

ISSEY MIYAKE
isseymiyake.com

JACQUEMUS
jacquemus.com

JENNIFER NEWMAN STUDIO
jennifernewman.com

JIL SANDER
jilsander.com

JOSEPH
joseph-fashion.com

JW ANDERSON
j-w-anderson.com

JUST RIGHT
justright.dk

LAMBERT ET FILS
lambertetfils.com

LEMAIRE
lemaire.fr

LEVI'S
levi.com

LOEWE
loewe.com

LUCCHESE
lucchese.com

LUISAVIAROMA
luisaviaroma.com

MAISON MARGIELA
maisonmargiela.com

MANSUR GAVRIEL
mansurgavriel.com

MARYAM NASSIR ZADEH
mnzstore.com

MYKITA
mykita.com

NET-A-PORTER
net-a-porter.com

NOMIA
nomia-nyc.com

OXOSI
oxosi.com

PROENZA SCHOULER
proenzaschouler.com

RACHEL COMEY
rachelcomey.com

RAINS
rains.com

SAINT-LOUIS
saint-louis.com

SCOUT LA
scoutla.net

STRING
string.se

SQUARESVILLE
squaresvillevintage.com

TIBI
tibi.com

TINA FREY
tinafreydesigns.com

VICTORIA BECKHAM
victoriabeckham.com

WANDA NYLON
wandanylon.fr

YOHJI YAMAMOTO
yohjiyamamoto.co.jp

ZERO + MARIA CORNEJO
zeromariacornejo.com

Behomm
Community

Home Exchange for Creatives and Design Lovers

TRAVEL STAYING FOR FREE AT HOMES OF CREATIVES

1. REGISTER WITH YOUR HOME.

2. CONTACT A HOME YOU LIKE. AGREE ON DATES.

3. STAY AT THEIR HOME FOR FREE WHILE THEY STAY AT YOURS.

3000 MEMBERS IN 66 COUNTRIES I BEHOMM.COM

ISSUE 25

Credits

P. 28
Artwork
Courtesy of *David Zwirner*

P. 36-37
Artwork
Pierre Charpin, collection of vases Torno Subito, 1998-2001, Limited edition, Galerie Kreo

P. 42
Artwork
Dan Flavin untitled (to *Barry, Mike, Chuck* and *Leonard*), 1972-1975 yellow and pink fluorescent light 8 ft. (244 cm) high, in a corridor measuring 8 ft. (244 cm) high and 8 ft. (244 cm) wide; length variable

P. 62-77
Production
Brooke McClelland

Hair
Fernando Torrent

Makeup
Yasuo Yoshikawa

Model
Alewya at Women Management

Casting Director
Lara Bonomo

Photography Assistant
Xander Ferreira

Styling Assistant
Barbara Ramos

P. 124-137
Production
Samuel Åberg

Model
Marine at The Squad

Casting Director
Sarah Bunter

Photography Assistants
Jean-Romain Pac
Antoine Bedos

Styling Assistant
Mara Gonzaléz Telmo

P. 138-145
From *How to Wrap Five Eggs* by *Hideyuki Oka* © 1965, 1972, 1975 by *Hideyuki Oka*. Photographs © Michikazu Sakai. Reprinted by arrangement with Weatherhill, an imprint of Shambhala Publications, Inc. Boulder, CO. *www. shambhala.com*

P. 146-155
An exhibition of *John T. Hill's* photographs of *Edna Lewis* will take place in the spring of 2018 in Chapel Hill, NC. The exhibition is curated by Ann Stewart Fine Art.
annstewartfineart.com.

P.157-158
Recipes first published in *The Futurist Cookbook* by *Filippo Tommaso Marinetti*, translated by *Suzanne Brill*. Courtesy Penguin Modern Classics

P. 168
Dress by Zero + Maria Cornejo

P. 180-181
Photograph
Courtesy of *Jean-Pierre Raynaud*

P. 184
Left Photograph:
Models
Giannina Oteto
Lela Maloney

Stylist
Lela Maloney

Hair and Makeup
Kristen Ruggiero

Right Photograph:
Stylist
Lela Maloney

Hair and Makeup
Elizabeth Lerman

Special Thanks
Mario Depicolzuane
Kim Donica
Grady O'Connor
Katelin Ross